# Assessing the Online Learner

JOSSEY-BASS GUIDES
TO ONLINE TEACHING AND LEARNING

# Assessing the Online Learner

## RESOURCES AND STRATEGIES FOR FACULTY

Rena Palloff and
Keith Pratt

Published by Jossey-Bass
A Wiley Imprint
989 Market Street, San Francisco, CA 94103-1741—www.josseybass.com



Jossey-Bass books and products are available through most bookstores. To contact Jossey-Bass directly call our Customer Care Department within the U.S. at 800-956-7739, outside the U.S. at 317-572-3986, or fax 317-572-4002.

Jossey-Bass also publishes its books in a variety of electronic formats. Some content that appears in print may not be available in electronic books.

**Library of Congress Cataloging-in-Publication Data**

Palloff, Rena M., 1950-
Assessing the online learner : resources and strategies for faculty / Rena M. Palloff and Keith Pratt.—1st ed.
p. cm.—(The Jossey-Bass higher and adult education series)
Includes bibliographical references and index.
ISBN 978-0-470-28386-8 (pbk.)
1. Distance education students—Rating of. 2. College students—Rating of. 3. Web-based instruction. 4. Internet in higher education. I. Pratt, Keith, 1947- II. Title.
LC5803.C65P34 2009
378.1'7344678—dc22

2008034931

Printed in the United States of America
FIRST EDITION

*PB Printing* 10 9 8 7 6 5 4

# CONTENTS

# LIST OF EXHIBITS

# PREFACE

Tests and quizzes have traditionally been used for assessing student performance in both face-to-face and online courses. Online instructors are finding, however, that this form of assessment may not adequately represent what the student has learned. They are searching for new ways to assess learner performance online that align with the teaching methods used in online courses. In addition, the use of tests and quizzes raises concern about the increased potential for cheating, particularly in the online environment, which does not allow instructors to easily monitor students taking tests.

The issue that plagues online instructors is finding ways to assess the activities in their courses that may not involve the use of tests and that are part of the course activities themselves. When assessment is built into a course activity, it is said to be in alignment with the course design. However, aligning course activities and desired outcomes with assessment of student performance in this way is a difficult task, and instructors are asking for help in learning how to do so. How can an instructor really know if students have met course objectives or have achieved content area competencies if tests and quizzes are not the main means of assessment? What other forms of assessment might be considered? This book addresses these questions and more. The goals of this book are to (1) critically evaluate concepts of assessment for the purpose of selecting those concepts that apply most directly to the online environment, (2) help readers develop working knowledge of assessment concepts, and (3) help them develop assessment techniques that do not involve the use of tests and quizzes for integration into an online course.

In addition to considering student assessment, many institutions are using course and program evaluation techniques that may or may not work well in the face-to-face environment, yet they are applying these in the online environment. The result is poor to no evaluation of what really goes on in the online classroom. Research on the topic of instructor performance online and the ability to evaluate that performance yields inconsistent results and lends little empirical data to this area (Tobin, 2004). Consequently, institutions are left with little on which to base their course evaluations. This book not only will assist instructors in developing more effective assessments in their classes but also will assist institutions in devising means by which to evaluate courses that include the student voice more effectively.

We have recently presented workshops at conferences and one four-week course on the topics of assessment and evaluation to packed houses. Faculty and instructional designers are clamoring for information about these topics and are convinced that tried and true methods of assessment and evaluation simply do not work well in the online environment. This viewpoint, coupled with escalating concerns about academic honesty online, has increased the importance of this topic.

## ABOUT THIS BOOK

This book is designed to help higher education professionals improve the practice of teaching and learning online, through improved techniques for the assessment of online learners and improved evaluation techniques for online courses. This concise, practical guide will help practitioners understand the basics of assessment online and apply those principles to creative assessment practices, such as the use of case studies, authentic assessments based in real-life application of concepts, and collaborative activities that move away from the traditional use of tests and quizzes—which generally determine the amount of information retained—and toward assessing *learning*. The design and use of rubrics as a technique for assessment, along with newer assessment techniques—such as wikis, blogs, and e-portfolios—will also be discussed.

The book is a very practical, process-focused work on the fundamental skills and tasks needed to design learner-focused assessments effectively in combination with other online instructional activities. The book is intended to provide guidance in the development of assessment and evaluation practices that can be realistically applied to the online learning environment in the higher education context. In other words, this work speaks to the real world of college or university professionals who are working in the online environment; it addresses the issues they face on a daily basis in course design and the alignment of good assessment with that design.

This book will help readers

- Know the differences between objectives, outcomes, and competencies and how these concepts are integrated into good assessment and evaluation practice
- Develop competence with the concept of learner-focused teaching and assessment
- Design rubrics and authentic assessments that accurately measure student achievement and learning and that directly relate to the activities in their courses
- Gain a repertoire of assessment tools that go beyond the use of tests and quizzes
- Develop authentic assessments that align with course content and provide direct application of course concepts for learners
- Use the online environment to their advantage when designing assessments
- Encourage students to develop skills in offering feedback by providing guidelines to good feedback and by modeling what is expected
- Incorporate feedback into the ongoing development of assessment and evaluation activities

## ORGANIZATION OF CONTENTS

As with previous books in the Jossey-Bass Guides to Online Teaching and Learning series, this book is designed to initially provide a bit of theory on which the work is based and then move quickly to practice and practice issues. The book is divided into two parts. Part One, Assessment Basics, provides that theoretical foundation. Chapter One reviews basic concepts and theories of assessment and assists the reader in understanding the development of competencies, outcomes, and objectives, along with their relationship to assessment. In addition, some references to learning theory—such as the Learning Pyramid, which stresses the concept that learners retain more knowledge by doing—are included to help the reader understand the assessment philosophy on which this book is built, which is a collaborative, action-oriented, learner-centered philosophy. This chapter also reviews the concept of learner-focused assessment and its importance in developing effective online assessment.

Chapter Two applies the assessment basics covered in Chapter One to the online environment. This chapter addresses the following questions: How do we empower learners to take responsibility for their learning in the online environment through good assessment? How can we bring the real world into the assessment of online learning? How can we incorporate higher-order thinking skills and reflection into online assessments? How can good online assessment practice help move students from basic knowledge acquisition and repetition to development as reflective practitioners? This chapter makes the point that good assessment can reduce the gap between what was taught and what was learned. We discuss rubric development as a means by which that gap can be bridged. The chapter also includes ways in which the online environment can be used for assessment advantage. The topic of online assessment also brings with it concerns about plagiarism and cheating. The chapter then turns to the following questions: How do we know that the student participating in the assessment is the one taking the course? If we give an exam, can the students be trusted to leave the book closed? How frequently does cheating happen online? How is plagiarism best addressed?

Chapter Three is devoted to the topics of course and program evaluation based on the concepts presented earlier in the book. We look at course and program evaluation as outgrowths of the development of competencies and outcomes, and we advocate for the use of competencies and outcomes as a basis for best practices in evaluation.

Part Two, The Assessment and Evaluation Toolkit, moves directly to practice by presenting individual assessment and evaluation techniques, along with suggestions for their implementation and use in an online course. The idea is to build a repertoire of assessment and evaluation skills that move beyond the tried and true and increase the realm of what is possible online. We close the book by offering additional resources that instructors or instructional designers will find helpful as they further develop assessment and evaluation practice.

## WHO WILL BENEFIT FROM READING THIS BOOK?

The primary audience for this book is higher education professionals, including faculty engaged in online teaching and instructional designers and other academic support staff involved in the development, design, and facilitation of online courses. A secondary audience includes other professionals in higher education who oversee the assessment and evaluation functions in online courses, such as department chairs, deans, and other administrators. Instructors who design and teach online courses, as well as instructional designers who develop online courses, will finish this book with an ability to design rubrics and authentic assessments that accurately measure student achievement and learning and directly relate to the activities in their courses. They will gain a repertoire of assessment tools that go beyond the use of tests and quizzes and an ability to evaluate online courses that goes beyond the usual "smile sheet" that students fill out at the end of the term. Administrators will finish this book with a greater appreciation of what is possible in online assessment and evaluation, and will be able to support greater experimentation with these techniques.

It is our hope that this book will demystify the topics of assessment and evaluation in the online environment, so instructors can feel confident that they have a better understanding of how and what students know when they leave a class. Although many of the techniques we discuss can be applied in face-to-face teaching as well, it is the use of these techniques online that is the focus of this book. Teaching online creates a unique environment for learning and thus calls for unique assessment measures that work well within it. We also hope to promote movement away from techniques that measure only what is memorized by a student and toward techniques that measure knowledge acquisition and application. To us, this is the measure of true learning.

# ACKNOWLEDGMENTS

The idea for this book arose from the intense interest of online faculty who were concerned about providing high-quality courses and programs for their students that were engaging and assessed to be the "right stuff." Their interest in what we had to say on this topic spurred us to create a book that would address their questions and needs. We say thank you to all who have attended our workshops on assessment over the last two years—we hope that this book answers your questions and more! We also want to thank Ed Leach of the League for Innovation in the Community College for recognizing that this is a critical topic and asking us to present it three times at various League conferences.

We cannot acknowledge too often the supportive and dedicated people at Jossey-Bass. Thanks to David Brightman, Erin Null, and Jessica Egbert for coming up with the idea for the Jossey-Bass Guides to Online Teaching and Learning series of books and for asking us to be the consulting editors on the project. Not only have we enjoyed writing our own contributions to the series, but we have also gained so much from working with the other talented authors who have contributed their work and ideas to it thus far.

Finally, thanks to the Fielding Graduate University and Judy Witt, the Dean of the School of Educational Leadership and Change, for helping us to launch the Teaching in the Virtual Classroom (TVC) program. The program gives us an opportunity to work with very talented instructors who are interested in improving the development and delivery of their online courses or who are moving into the online environment and want to do so with greater knowledge, skill, and ability. Most of all, we thank our participants—the "students" in the TVC program—for their contributions to our ongoing learning and their generosity in allowing us to include their wonderful activities as examples in this book.

Virtual hugs to you all! We cannot thank you enough.

Rena Palloff
Alameda, California

Keith Pratt
Pineville, Missouri

# THE AUTHORS

*Rena M. Palloff* is a managing partner of Crossroads Consulting Group, working with institutions, organizations, and corporations interested in the development of online distance learning and training programs, and conducting faculty development training and coaching. In addition, Dr. Palloff has consulted extensively in health care, academic settings, and addiction treatment for over twenty years. She is faculty at Fielding Graduate University, in the master's degree program in Organizational Management and Development and also in the School of Educational Leadership and Change. She is also adjunct faculty at Capella University in the School of Human Services. Additionally, Dr. Palloff has taught classes on organizational behavior and management and leadership on an adjunct basis for the International Studies Program at Ottawa University in Ottawa, Kansas, in various sites throughout the Pacific Rim, and as core faculty at John F. Kennedy University in Holistic Studies.

Dr. Palloff received a bachelor's degree in sociology from the University of Wisconsin-Madison and a master's degree in social work from the University of Wisconsin-Milwaukee. She holds a master's degree in organizational development and a Ph.D. in human and organizational systems from Fielding Graduate University.

*Keith Pratt* began his government career as a computer systems technician with the U.S. Air Force in 1967. He served in various positions, including supervisor of computer systems maintenance, chief of the Logistics Support Branch, chief of the Telecommunications Branch, and superintendent of the Secure Telecommunications Branch. After leaving the air force, Pratt held positions as registrar and faculty (Charter College), director (Chapman College), and trainer and consultant (The Growth Company). As an adjunct faculty member at Wayland Baptist University and at the University of Alaska, Pratt taught courses in communications, business, management, organizational theories, and computer technology. He was assistant professor in the International Studies Program and chair of the Management Information Systems program, on the main campus and overseas, at Ottawa University in Ottawa, Kansas. He currently teaches online at Fielding Graduate University and Wayland Baptist University, and is Lead Faculty Mentor for Professional Development at Northcentral University.

Pratt graduated from Wayland Baptist University with a dual degree in business administration and computer systems technology. He has a master's degree in human resource management (with honors) from Chapman University, a master's degree in organizational development, a Ph.D. in human and organizational systems from Fielding Graduate University, and an honorary doctorate of science from Moscow State University.

Palloff and Pratt are managing partners in Crossroads Consulting Group. Since 1994 they have collaboratively conducted pioneering research and training in the emerging areas of online group facilitation, face-to-face and online community building, program planning and development of distance learning programs, and management and supervision of online academic programs. In conjunction with Fielding Graduate University, they developed and are core faculty in the Teaching in the Virtual Classroom academic certificate program, designed to assist faculty in becoming effective online facilitators and course developers.

# Assessing the Online Learner

**PART ONE**

# Assessment Basics

chapter
ONE

# How Do We Know They Know?

There is no doubt that online learning and the development of online courses is proliferating. The convenience of working online has proven to be very attractive to students and instructors alike. The ability to work from the comfort of home or a dorm room, the elimination of traffic and parking problems, the elimination of child-care problems, and the ability to attend class at any time have been driving forces in its popularity. Convenience, convenience, convenience has become the mantra for both students and instructors. Convenience does not make online learning any less rigorous than its face-to-face cousin; in fact, the combination of rigor and convenience seems to strengthen its appeal.

Despite its popularity, online learning is not without its challenges. As instructors are finding their way in the online environment and paying more attention to good course design and delivery, they are discovering that traditional forms of assessment of student work—such as tests and quizzes—that served them well in the face-to-face classroom may not work quite as well online. Milam, Voorhees, and Bedard-Voorhees (2004) note, "The online paradigm holds that learning itself may be different in the online environment and, if that is true, then the methodology for measuring it should also be different or should measure those things that are, in fact, different" (p. 74). Given that delivering education online is changing the landscape of learning, bringing with it approaches and techniques that are not necessarily used in the face-to-face classroom, doesn't it make sense that the ways in which we assess student learning and evaluate courses should change as well? Furthermore, along with the dramatic increase in online offerings and concern about effective assessment has come increased concern about academic honesty, raising questions like these:

- Is the student who has enrolled in the course the student who is participating, taking exams and quizzes, writing papers, and so on?
- How do I, as the instructor, know that students really understand and can apply the material I'm teaching if I can't see them?
- How can I ensure that students won't cheat on exams or other assessments in my online course?
- How can I deal with plagiarism online?

Although it has brought convenience, the online environment has also brought additional concerns and a call to move beyond traditional means of identifying what students know during and at the end of a course. Our basic philosophy and approach to assessment may not change, but the techniques we use to get there are likely to be different.

## DEVELOPING STANDARDS OF ASSESSMENT

Dunn, Morgan, O'Reilly, and Parry (2004) note that one of the problems with developing student-centered, authentic assessment policies is that assessment is a value-laden process, no matter how assessors attempt to standardize it. This problem does not improve when we move online, as it lies in the need to develop benchmarks of student completion of what the authors term "performable learning outcomes" (p. 25) that align with the knowledge base of the particular content area as well as the profession it serves. They further note the concern that assessment needs to be "about appropriate levels of skill and knowledge and about appropriate analytical, methodological, and theoretical frames of reference and their applications. These kinds of professional understandings are not necessarily explicit features of academic professions" (p. 26). Dunn, Parry, and Morgan (2002) further note that standards vary with the profession. The so-called soft sciences, such as the humanities and social and behavioral sciences, demand interpretations of the theory that undergirds those disciplines.

In these fields, assessment criteria cannot be too precise or rigid, as building arguments that provide new insights is the benchmark of good performance. In the hard sciences, however, assessment generally consists of application of existing knowledge and skill. Although the development of new knowledge is valued, it is the skill with which the student applies what is learned that is important. The authors note, "Competent assessment depends upon the extent to which disciplinary conventions and values are highlighted through assessment criteria" (Implications for setting standards and making judgments, para. 6).

It behooves instructors and other assessors, then, to become knowledgeable about best practices in assessment and how to develop standards and benchmarks based on both content and the professional context in which that content resides. The same is true with the evaluation of online courses and programs—what are the best practices in course and program evaluation? How do those practices align with what is demanded in the fields to which the courses and programs relate?

To tackle this sometimes complicated topic, we will first review some of the assessment basics that should guide assessment practice in any environment and thus form a foundation of best practices in assessment and course or program evaluation in any environment—online, face-to-face, or hybrid. We will then turn to a discussion of learning activities in courses and how those relate to assessment, accompanied by a discussion of learner-focused teaching and assessment.

## GETTING DOWN TO THE BASICS

Magennis and Farrell (2005) offer this definition of teaching: "Teaching is taken to mean a set of activities that makes learning possible" (p. 45). Fink (n.d.) further notes that teaching is not about providing instruction, but about producing learning. Learning, according to Fink, is defined in terms of change—for learning to occur, the learner needs to experience some form of change. Although this sounds very simple to understand on the surface, teaching activities and their relationship to learning and assessment are actually quite complex. Before an instructor can embark on the development of good online activities and assessments, he or she must have a solid understanding of how assessment fits into the scheme of course development as well as the components it comprises. Instructors need to understand learning outcomes, their importance in the learning process, their development, and how to achieve them. The components that make up course design are often referred to as *competencies*, *outcomes*, and *objectives.* Although these terms are likely familiar to those reading this book, instructors often do not accurately differentiate among them. There are differences among these terms, however, and the assessment of each differs. The differences are as follows:

- Objectives: What students will *learn*, generally at the end of a unit of study
- Outcomes: What students will be able to *know or do*, generally at the end of a course
- Competencies: How students *demonstrate knowledge or skill acquisition*, generally at the end of a program of study

The three form a set of building blocks from the program level to the unit level of a course. Competencies form the foundation, with outcomes and objectives flowing from them. Exhibit 1.1 illustrates this configuration.

**Exhibit 1.1**
**Course Development Model**

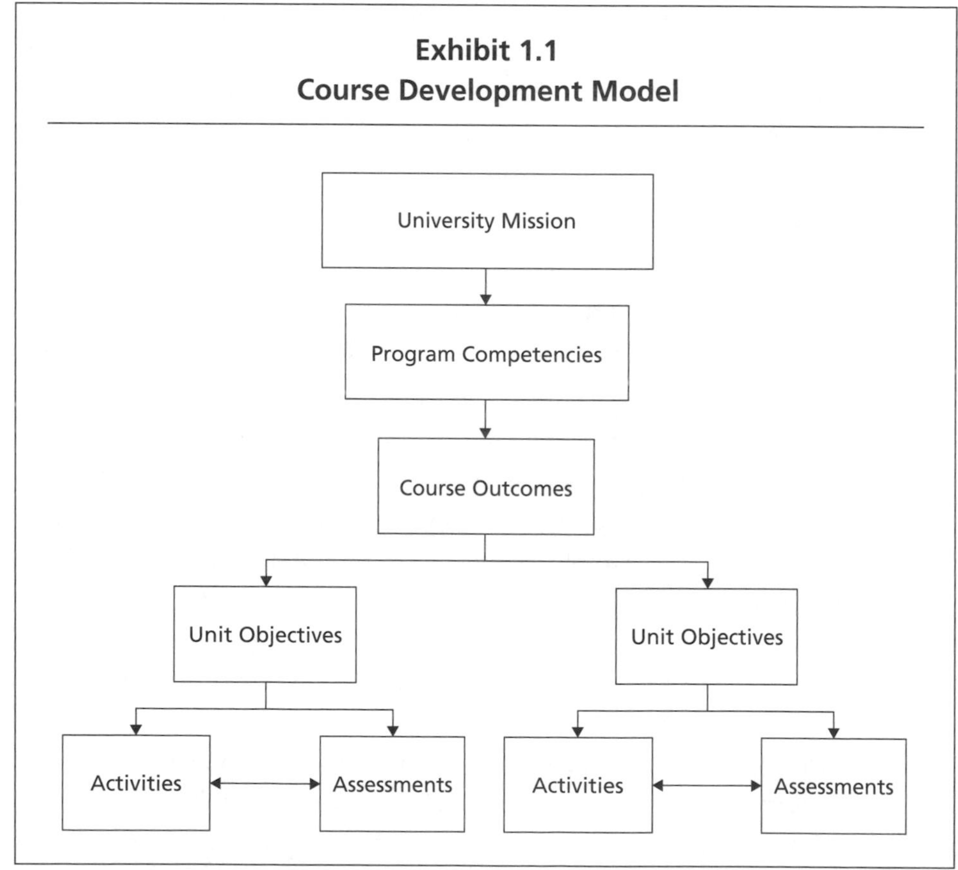

We will now look at how these work in the design of a course for delivery in any medium.

## Competencies

Jones, Voorhees, and Paulson (2002) define competencies as "the combination of skills, abilities, and knowledge needed to perform a specific task" (p. 7). Competencies support the dynamic link between knowing and expressing. They are developmental, which partially explains why competencies can be defined at a programmatic level—by the time students complete a program of study, what knowledge, skills, or abilities do we hope they will possess? When they leave our institution, regardless of their majors, what do we want to see them be or do? Competencies assume that students will gain greater knowledge of who they are as learners as they complete a program of study or take numerous courses within one institution, regardless of means of delivery. It is through a focus on competencies that Fink's (n.d.) notion of significant change in the learner's life comes into play. Establishing competencies assumes that learners will enter the program at one point, experience learning opportunities that allow them to change and grow as learners and professionals, and exit the program in a very different place from where they began. There is an underlying assumption that the change will be lasting and significant to the learner.

The establishment of competencies provides the first step in a cycle of good course design. Dunn, Morgan, O'Reilly, and Parry (2004) discuss the importance of ensuring alignment when it comes to good assessment practice, meaning that any outcomes or learning objectives developed at the course level need to reflect the competencies that have been determined at the program level. They describe an even broader configuration, such as the one we presented in Exhibit 1.1, that begins with the university mission and links that to the desired attributes of graduates from the institution. This informs the development of competencies, which then inform the development of course outcomes that should directly relate to the determined competencies. Course outcomes, according to Dunn et al., should reflect required disciplinary skills and knowledge, along with a reflection of the values and traditions of that discipline. Although it appears complicated at first, as an instructor develops a course, he or she should be able to map the learning objectives for one unit of study; for example, to the larger program competencies that the institution is attempting to ensure that students achieve.

Another influence on the development of competencies is that many disciplines—such as computer science, management, and education—have established competencies for practice either through professional organizations that oversee that discipline or at the state or even federal level. The example in Exhibit 1.2 is an excerpt from a set of teacher competencies used in undergraduate teacher training programs delivered in the state of New Mexico. Academic programs designed to prepare teachers to teach in that state would need to somehow incorporate these competencies into program design.

Thus, the development of competencies also provides groundwork for program evaluation, a topic we will discuss in Chapter Three. With the concept of alignment as a foundation, we can now look at what it takes to design a course that incorporates these principles and wherein assessment is also in alignment.

## Outcomes

Once competencies are established, the next level of focus should be the development of course outcomes. Course outcomes are important in that they help students learn more effectively and make it clear what students can expect to gain from taking the course. Additionally, they help instructors to design materials

**Exhibit 1.2**
**Sample Professional Competencies**

New Mexico Teacher Competencies for Licensure Levels I, II, and III Assessment Criteria *Benchmarks*

New Mexico is one of the most diverse states in the nation, and this diversity is reflected in the strengths and needs of New Mexico's students. The ability of a highly qualified teacher to address the learning needs of all New Mexico's students—including those students who learn differently as a result of disability, culture, language, or socioeconomic status—forms the framework for the New Mexico Teacher Competencies for Licensure Levels I, II, and III Assessment Criteria Benchmarks.

**I. The Teacher Accurately Demonstrates Knowledge of the Content Area and Approved Curriculum.**

| Provisional Teacher: Level I | Professional Teacher: Level II | Master Teacher: Level III |
|---|---|---|
| A. Utilizes and enhances approved curriculum. | A. Enhances and extends approved curriculum. | A. Contributes to the refinement and development of the approved curriculum. |
| B. Gives clear explanations relating to lesson content and procedures. | B. Gives clear explanations relating to lesson content and procedures. | B. Provides clear explanations relating to lesson content and procedures in multiple ways and is aware of knowledge and preconceptions that students can bring to the subject. |
| C. Communicates accurately in the content area. | C. Communicates accurately in the content area. | C. Communicates accurately in the content area and can create multiple paths to the subject matter. |
| D. Shows interrelatedness of one content area to another. | D. Integrates other subjects into the content curriculum. | D. Can articulate to students the interrelatedness of the disciplines. |

**IV. The Teacher Comprehends the Principles of Student Growth, Development, and Learning, and Applies Them Appropriately.**

| Provisional Teacher: Level I | Professional Teacher: Level II | Master Teacher: Level III |
|---|---|---|
| A. Instructs students in the use of cognitive thinking skills, such as critical thinking, problem solving, divergent thinking, inquiry, and decision making. | A. Consistently integrates the use of cognitive thinking skills, such as critical thinking, problem solving, divergent thinking, inquiry, and decision making, into instruction. | A. Consistently integrates the use of cognitive thinking skills, such as critical thinking, problem solving, divergent thinking, inquiry, and decision making, into instruction. |

(*Continued*)

**Exhibit 1.2 (*Continued*)**

| Provisional Teacher: Level I | Professional Teacher: Level II | Master Teacher: Level III |
|---|---|---|
| B. Uses teaching techniques that address student learning levels, rates, and styles. | B. Adapts teaching techniques to accommodate a range of student learning levels, rates, styles, and special needs. | B. Selects the most effective teaching techniques to address a variety of student learning levels, rates, styles, and needs, as well as diverse interests and backgrounds. |
| C. Uses materials and media that address student learning levels, rates, and styles. | C. Adapts materials and media to address a range of student learning levels, rates, styles, and special needs. | C. Selects the most effective materials and media to address a variety of student learning levels, rates, styles, and needs. |
| D. Uses resources, such as community service agencies, school personnel, and parents, to meet student learning levels, rates, and styles. | D. Selects from a variety of community service agencies, specialized school personnel, and parents to address different learning levels, rates, styles, and needs. | D. Integrates community resources, service agencies, other school personnel, parents, and community members into the curriculum. |

*Source:* New Mexico Teacher Competencies, 9/10/2003. Retrieved on June 10, 2007 from [http://www.teachnm.org/nm_teacher_competencies.html].

more effectively and to more precisely describe what an activity is designed to do. Finally, they assist in determining assessments for measuring student performance in the course. Outcomes are generally written to cover four areas of learning:

- *Knowledge*—Content, topics, and the like
- *Cognitive skills*—What students are expected to *do* with the content (based on Bloom's Taxonomy, which we discuss a bit later in this chapter)
- *Subject-specific skills*—Professional skills, motor skills, and so on

- *Key skills*—Specifically tied to the competencies established for the program of study

Well-written outcomes contain three parts:

- *Behavior*—Outcome described in performance terms
- *Criterion*—How well or how often a learner must perform to be judged adequate
- *Conditions*—The conditions under which the student is expected to perform

When we look at outcomes in this way, their relationship to assessment becomes clearer. Any time a course developer writes an outcome, he or she should ask, "Does this outcome *clearly communicate* the *desired behavior to be achieved*?" The behavior, then, becomes the focus of assessment. The following example breaks down what we have just discussed in terms of developing a possible outcome for a math class:

- *Condition: Given a set of data, the student will be able to compute the standard deviation.*
- *Behavior:* The student will be able to compute the standard deviation.
- *Criterion (implied):* The number computed will be correct.

In this example, the behavior to be achieved is clear, and the assessment takes into account not only the correct answer but also the process by which the answer was calculated. The student then understands that the process in this case is as important as the product, as that is what is communicated through the course outcomes.

Another important task in writing outcomes is the selection of language that is clear and indicates the desired behavior from students. Verbs that indicate action should be used. Vague verbs, such as *understand*, *learn*, or *know about* should be avoided in favor of such verbs as *describe*, *discuss*, *restate*, *analyze*, *synthesize*, and the like. In summary, to be effective, good learning outcomes are

- Consistent with the goals of the curriculum (competencies to be achieved)
- Clearly stated
- Measurable
- Realistic and doable

- Appropriate to the level of the learner
- Focused on the important results desired at the end of the course rather than minutia

## Elements of Good Course Design

Just as with the development of competencies and outcomes, and the use of them as a foundation, good course design or development begins with the end in mind. In other words, what is it that we want learners to be able to know or do at the end of the course that aligns with what we want them to be able to perform professionally when they leave the program? These course outcomes should be both measurable and observable in student behavior or application of course material. With outcomes as the foundation, we can then begin to create a cycle of course design that includes determining who our students are—what characteristics are they likely to posses? How much knowledge about this course will they bring with them at the start? Is this a foundational course or one that comes further along in a sequence of courses on the topic? Knowing who our students are and how they learn—a topic we will cover a bit later in this chapter—helps us to design a course that is learner focused and centered—a hallmark of good online course development.

Once we have a good understanding of what we want to accomplish in the course and to whom the course will be delivered, we can begin to tackle the task of laying out the course in units and determining what will be accomplished in each. The goal here is to link the unit objectives with the overall outcomes of the course—in other words, how will this unit serve to meet course outcomes? The objectives for each unit should drive the development of activities—what can we ask students to *do* that demonstrates they have achieved the objectives for the unit and eventually the outcomes for the course? Every course activity (perhaps with the exception of reading assignments) should have an assessment linked to it that demonstrates mastery of concepts within the unit and also links to demonstration of mastery of course outcomes. Exhibit 1.3 illustrates the cycle we have just described.

Following Exhibit 1.3 is an example of a graduate-level course in a master's program in organizational management, written and designed by one of the authors, that demonstrates the alignment of competencies with outcomes with unit learning objectives. Only one unit is presented in this example. However, the alignment should be seen in all units of the course.

**Exhibit 1.3**
**Cycle of Course Design**

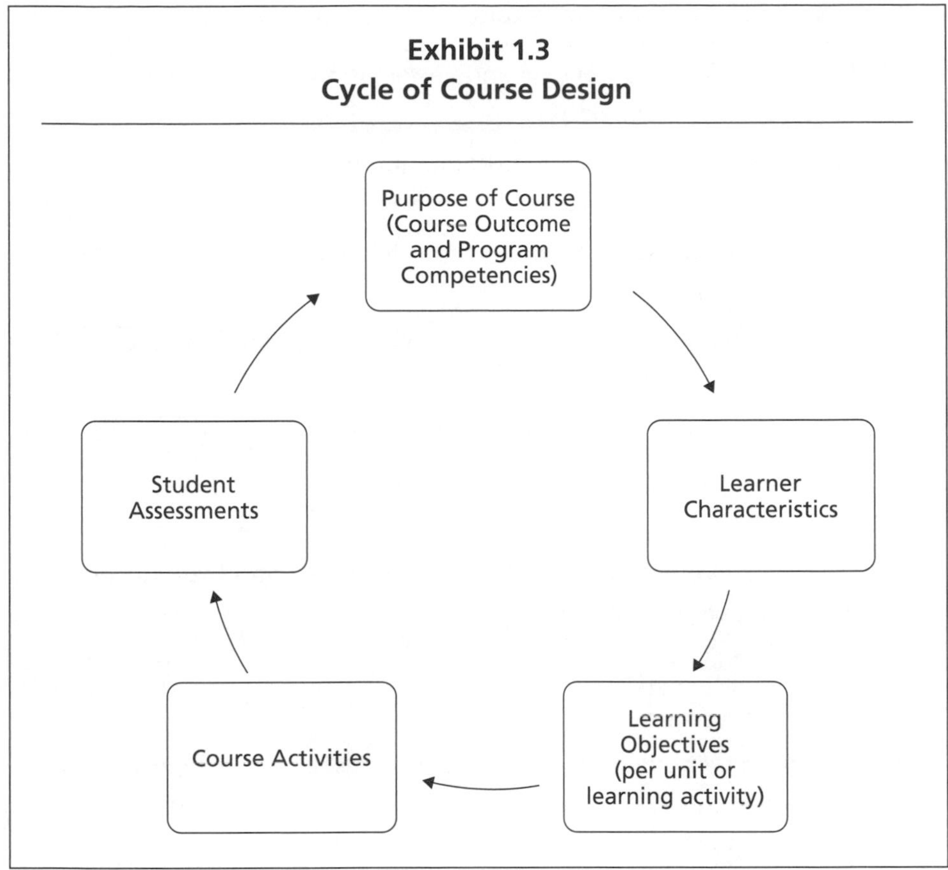


## COURSE DESCRIPTION—RESISTANCE TO CHANGE

This course provides an understanding of change and resistance to change from individual, group, and organizational levels. It focuses on the signs and symptoms of resistance and how to appreciate resistance as a catalyst and creative force. We will examine the issues of power, politics, fear, and loss often associated with resistance to change and will emphasize resistance to change in the context of transitional and transformational change. We will explore different theories of change and techniques and interventions for working with resistance in various organizational settings. In addition, we will explore means by which change can be accomplished without engendering resistance.

Some of the questions we will explore in this course are

1. How do various models of change affect individual, team, and organizational behaviors?
2. What are the key signals, symptoms, and underlying causes of resistance?
3. How can resistance be viewed and understood as a creative and catalytic force?
4. How can change processes be initiated and managed so that resistance does not occur?
5. How do I recognize and personally respond to change and resistance?
6. What interventions are effective when dealing with resistance to change?
7. What is the role of the consultant, team leader, and team members in dealing with resistance?

**Program Competencies:**

The program's "golden threads"—values, research, and professional practices—are integrated into our curriculum and our approach to professional development. The following key theoretical concepts and organizational practices are woven into every OMD course.

- Application of adult learning principles, collaborative dialogue, shared leadership, and integration of diverse perspectives to develop personal and organizational competencies in human systems
- Development of sustainable organizations that provide nourishment for the lives of their members, customers, and the communities and environments they influence
- Safe and supportive learning environment that embraces creativity, reflection, diversity, culture, systems thinking, and the professional practice of organization management and development in all manner of institutions and organizations
- Scholar/practitioner approach that values the practical application of organizational theory, critical thinking, and scholarly writing

- Student-centered curriculum that builds on student strengths and leadership qualities

**Course Outcomes:**

- Ability to access and utilize change management techniques in the workplace
- Ability to design interventions to address resistance to change in an organizational setting
- Gaining of an understanding of self as an instrument in the change process
- Appreciation of the historical and contemporary concepts of resistance to change and change management
- Demonstrated understanding of change and resistance to change at individual, group, and organizational levels
- Appreciation of resistance as a catalyst and creative force
- Demonstrated understanding of the role of change agents in the change process

**Unit Objectives:**

- Present the similarities, differences, strengths, and limitations of traditional models of organizational change management in terms of engendering or reducing resistance.
- Assess practical applications of the models at an organizational level.
- Research, explore, and present new models of change and resistance at the individual and organizational levels.

**Assessments:**

- Assessment 1—Review the change scenario provided in the Course Resources area. You will be assigned a partner for this activity. With your partner, present and discuss the one theory from the reading that you think best applies to this scenario and is most likely to reduce resistance to change, along with your rationale for why you think this is the best approach. Develop a consolidated response and post it to the discussion board. Respond to one other team's response.

- Assessment 2—Each of you will do a library or internet search (or both) for an approach to resistance from a field other than business (such as psychology or education). Present that approach in a brief essay and then discuss its application to the same scenario you discussed with your partner.

---

An example of how the program competencies might be mapped to the outcomes, objectives, and assessments in this example is shown in Exhibit 1.4.

The mapping of competencies to outcomes, objectives, and assessments should be transparent to anyone who looks at the course, including students. In fact, some academic institutions note the mapping in the syllabus by numbering the outcomes and then listing the outcome numbers in each unit so that students can more easily see how the unit assignments relate to the outcomes. Simply putting that in print is not enough, however. Brian Trautman, an online instructor, talks about his strategy for helping students understand the connection between the outcomes and the weekly activities in the course:

> The mapping to course outcomes in the syllabus (and then again in the introduction to each week's discussion) is an interesting concept and practice. While I am not sure new students (at least those new to online learning . . .) see the significance and value, and while I am not sure most spend the time to tie the outcomes to the material and discussion, I do my best each week to incorporate each outcome into at least a few discussion questions/responses, which is to say that I use the language of the TCOs [Terminal Course Objectives] to communicate questions and follow up responses. Then, at the end of each week, I typically post a question along the lines of, "Are there any questions about how this week's readings and discussion correspond to our highlighted TCOs for the week?" I think this helps.
>
> —*Brian*

When assessment aligns with competencies, outcomes, learning objectives, and course activities, the task of assessment becomes less cumbersome and student satisfaction with the learning process increases (Morgan & O'Reilly, 1999). Additionally, students' understanding of the purpose of the course in their overall program of learning grows significantly.

**Exhibit 1.4**
**Map of Competencies to Outcomes, Objectives, and Assessments**

| Program Competencies | Course Outcomes | Unit Learning Objectives | Assessment |
|---|---|---|---|
| Development of sustainable organizations that provide nourishment for the lives of their members, customers, and the communities and environments they influence. | Ability to design interventions to address resistance to change in an organizational setting. | Assess practical applications of the models at an organizational level | *Assessment 1*—Review the change scenario provided in the Course Resources area. You will be assigned a partner for this activity. With your partner, present and discuss the one theory from the reading that you think best applies to this scenario and is most likely to reduce resistance to change, along with your rationale for why you think this is the best approach. Develop a consolidated response and post it to the discussion board. Respond to one other team's response. |

## Activities That Promote Knowledge Retention

In thinking about designing assessments, it is also important to keep in mind how people learn and what activities contribute to knowledge retention. Kolitch and Dean (1999) suggest two theoretical models of teaching: the *transmission model*, in which the instructor imparts information and the learner absorbs it, and what these authors call the *engaged critical model*, in which teaching and learning are seen as a creative dialogue. The critical model concerns itself more squarely with the function of learning and is learner focused, whereas the transmission model is more focused on teaching and is instructor focused. Much of what exists in traditional assessments is based on the transmission model. The forms of instruction that happen online, however, are more in line with the engaged critical model.

The Learning Pyramid, developed by National Training Laboratories in Bethel, Maine, in the early 1960s, provides information about the progression of activities that contribute to knowledge acquisition and retention, and helps to inform good assessment. Additionally, the top levels of the pyramid reflect the transmission model of teaching, while the lower levels reflect the engaged critical model. It follows then that instruction based in the engaged critical model should use assessments that align with that form of teaching. The lower levels of the pyramid include discussions, practicing by doing—also known as *authentic assessment*—and teaching others. Using these activities as assessments promotes learner-centered instruction, wherein the construction of knowledge and meaning is paramount.

From reviewing the pyramid and considering the theoretical concept of engaged critical teaching, it becomes clear that what we call authentic assessment—that is, assessment that encourages learners to actually *do* something to demonstrate knowledge acquisition rather than taking a test or quiz—is not only a better indicator of knowledge acquisition but also more likely to align with outcomes and competencies, and it also contributes to the retention of knowledge gained.

Barnett (1990) notes that in higher education students should be able to (1) gain deep understanding of concepts, (2) critique concepts, (3) conduct that critique in front of others, (4) perform independent inquiry, (5) self-reflect, and (6) engage in open dialogue. The transmission model does not allow for the development of learners in this way, nor does reliance on multiple choice or true/false testing as assessments. Consequently, in consideration of how students learn and retain knowledge, when instructors are designing course activities and their related assessments they need to focus their efforts at the lower levels of the learning pyramid.

Keeping the focus on outcomes when developing learning activities helps instructors to

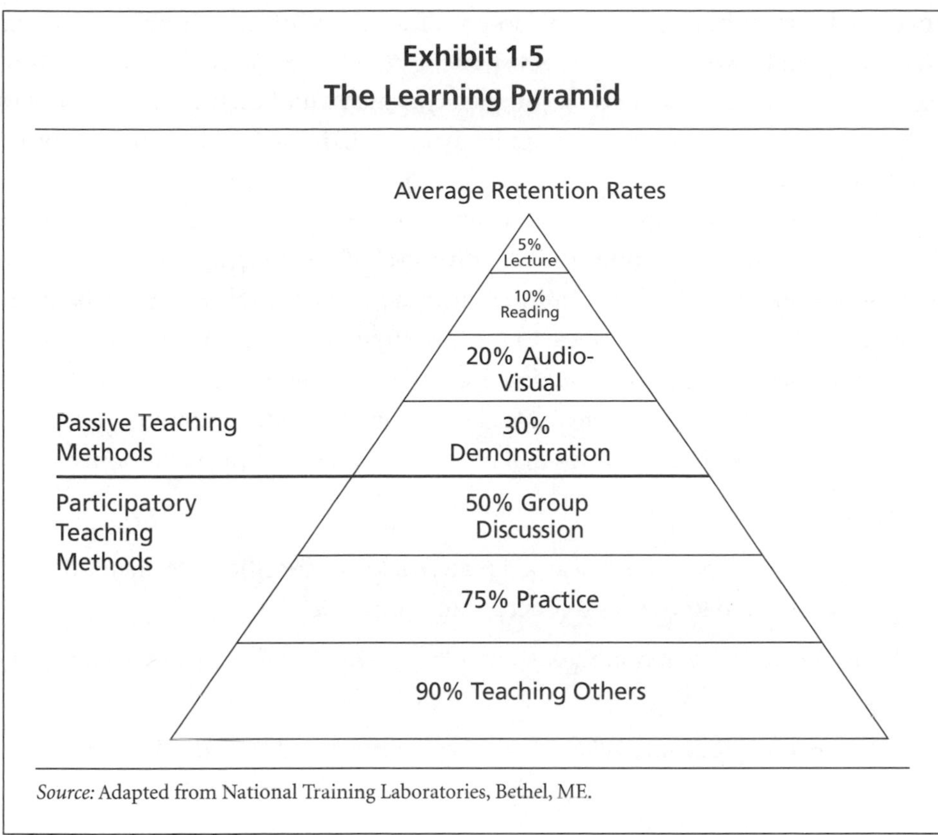


**Exhibit 1.5**
**The Learning Pyramid**

*Source:* Adapted from National Training Laboratories, Bethel, ME.

- Select content
- Develop instructional strategy
- Develop instructional materials
- Construct assessments that align with the competencies

## Bloom's Taxonomy

Outcomes and learning activities are generally created with an eye toward moving students from basic levels of understanding of concepts to the ability to apply those concepts in a professional or academic setting, to the ability to evaluate the concepts once they have been applied—in other words, from what are considered to be lower-order skills to higher-order skills. To accomplish this, many educators have turned to Bloom's Taxonomy of educational objectives (Bloom & Krathwohl, 1956) for assistance. Bloom's Taxonomy lays out levels of outcomes in terms of increasing complexity, which build on one another, and to which activities and assessments can be mapped. Exhibit 1.6 illustrates the levels in the taxonomy.

To write course outcomes and assessment activities that match Bloom's levels, an instructor would determine the cognitive level of the desired outcome and then choose action verbs that measure the outcome at that level. It cannot be overstressed that verb choice is critical to the measurement of outcomes. Too often we have seen the verbs *discuss* or *understand* used in outcomes that should address higher-order skills. To assist the reader in developing good, measurable outcomes, we offer examples of action verbs that measure each level of the taxonomy.

**Knowledge:**

- Ability to recall previously learned material; know specific facts, methods, and procedures; and know basic concepts and principles
- Verbs: *define, label, recall, repeat, order, list, quote, match, state, recognize, identify, recite*
- Answers the questions: *Who, what, when, where, how? How do you define . . . ?*

**Exhibit 1.6**
**Bloom's Taxonomy**

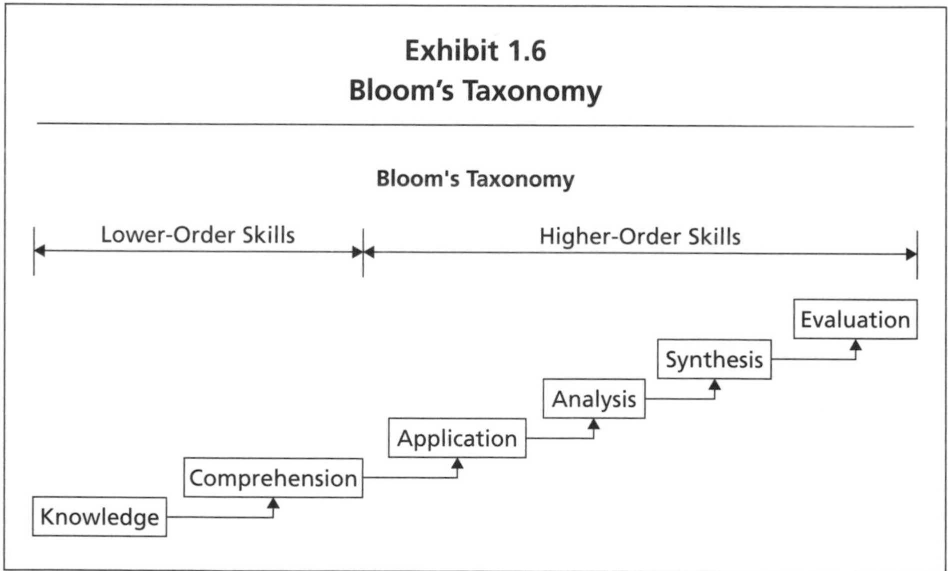

- Possible assignments or assessments: reading and discussion of activities, tests, and quizzes; summaries of reading; homework assignments derived from reading the text or delivery of content, such as listening to lectures or reviewing web pages

**Comprehension:**

- Ability to understand the meaning of material, interpret charts and graphs, estimate future consequences implied in the data
- Verbs: *describe, discuss, restate, summarize, paraphrase, report, review, understand, explain, identify, locate, express, recognize*
- Answers the questions: *What are the main ideas? How would you summarize? Give examples of . . .*
- Possible assignments or assessments: summaries that call for paraphrasing of material, oral or written presentations, internet or library search activities, WebQuests

**Application:**

- Ability to use learned information in new situations, problem solving, solutions that have "best answers"; to demonstrate correct usage of procedures; to apply laws or theories to practical situations
- Verbs: *assess, demonstrate, examine, distinguish, establish, show, report, implement, determine, produce, solve, draw, interpret, provide, use, utilize, write, illustrate, operate, dramatize, sketch, employ*
- Answers the questions: *How is xx an example of yy? How is xx related to yy? Why is xx significant?*
- Possible assignments or assessments: demonstrations; research papers that apply concepts; development of websites or wikis; fishbowl activities; authentic assessments that call for application of material to real-life situations, such as case studies or simulations

**Analysis:**

- Ability to identify component parts of knowledge, to understand its structure and composition, to recognize logical fallacies in reasoning, to make distinctions between facts and inferences

- Verbs: *analyze, illustrate, discriminate, differentiate, distinguish, examine, question, infer, support, prove, test, experiment, categorize, write, appraise, calculate, criticize, compare, contrast, relate*
- Answers the questions: *What are the parts or features of xx? Classify according to . . . ? Outline/diagram . . . How does xx compare or contrast with yy? What evidence is there for . . . ?*
- Possible assignments or assessments: experiments, critiques, essays comparing and contrasting concepts, research assignments that require supporting materials beyond assigned texts, debates, blogs

**Synthesis:**

- Ability to creatively apply knowledge to new areas, to integrate new knowledge, to write a well-argued paper or speech, to propose a research design to test a hypothesis
- Verbs: *compile, categorize, generate, negotiate, reconstruct, reorganize, revise, validate, organize, plan, propose, set up, write, substitute, initiate, express, compare, modify, design, create, build, devise, integrate, compose, assemble, manage*
- Answers the questions: *What would you infer or predict from . . . ? What ideas can you add to . . . ? How would you create or design . . . ? What might happen if you . . . ? What solutions would you suggest?*
- Possible assignments or assessments: small group projects, jigsaw activities, proposals, wikis

**Evaluation:**

- Ability to judge the value of evidence or material for a given purpose
- Verbs: *appraise, criticize, assess, argue, justify, defend, interpret, support, estimate, evaluate, critique, review, write, judge, measure, choose, value, compute, revise, score, select*
- Answers the questions: *Do you agree that . . . ? What do you think about . . .? What is the most important . . . ? Prioritize and give a rationale for . . . Decision making—what is your rationale . . .? Criteria for assessing . . .*
- Possible assignments or assessments: debates, critiques, action research projects, peer review of papers

This discussion and illustration of how outcomes and assessments might be linked to Bloom's Taxonomy are not meant to ascribe judgment by indicating that all outcomes and assessments should be written at the highest levels of synthesis and evaluation. Instead, the instructor should once again think about what it is that he or she wants students to be able to perform, think, know, or do at the end of the course, and then link those thoughts to the appropriate level in Bloom's Taxonomy that they represent. For example, introductory courses may have outcomes and assessments that do not go beyond the comprehension level, whereas courses that are taken by students who are further along in their studies are likely to contain outcomes and activities that may span the taxonomy. When recognized as a developmental process, the use of the taxonomy can be helpful in determining outcomes that are appropriate to the level of the course (meaning introductory to advanced) as well as the level of the learners.

## Grading

When the focus of a course remains on outcomes and when assignments are designed to elicit the kind of learning that is desired, the task of grading becomes much easier. Additionally, the assignments should (1) align with the type of desired learning, (2) be reasonable in terms of workload, (3) be strategically placed in the course, and (4) sustain ongoing learning. Furthermore, directions for completing the assessment need to be clear and unambiguous to minimize student confusion and maximize successful assignment completion. Walvoord and Anderson (1998) state, "Students will complete the assignment they think you made, not the assignment you actually made. With sketchy or ambiguous instructions, you run the risk of having students draw off previous learning that may not be relevant or desirable in your situation" (p. 38).

Faculty often note that they want to help students develop their ability to analyze, synthesize, and think critically—the higher-order skills of Bloom's Taxonomy. However, the assignments in a course may not align with those goals, and consequently the task of assessment and the assigning of a grade become difficult. Walvoord and Anderson (1998) further recommend using grading scales or rubrics (which we will discuss in more depth in Chapter Two) that are assignment-specific and designed with criteria that are highly explicit. When students understand what is expected of them in the assignment, the final product received matches instructor expectations, and final grades can be assessed using the criteria developed for that assignment. Walvoord and Anderson further note that ongoing formative feedback on student work is much more valuable than waiting to provide extensive feedback on the final assignment. By providing feedback throughout the course or on pieces of large assignments as they are completed, the instructor acts as a coach, moving students toward the goal of achieving higher-order thinking skills. Having clear expectations and grading criteria creates consistency in grading and helps to engage learners in their own learning process, as they know what they are aiming for and can assess their own progress along the way.

## LEARNER-FOCUSED TEACHING

Another concept to keep in mind when thinking about appropriate assessment is learner-focused teaching. Maryellen Weimer (2002), in her book *Learner-Centered Teaching*, discusses the benefits of keeping a learner focus in a class. Huba and Freed (2000) further note that in a learner-centered paradigm, students construct knowledge by gathering together and synthesizing information by using inquiry, communication, critical thinking, and problem solving. The instructor's role is to facilitate the process, and instructors and students together assess learning, much as we have described in our philosophy of learning community–based online teaching. In this way, teaching and learning are intertwined and the results are best assessed through papers, projects, performance of authentic application activities, portfolios, and the like. The benefits of such practice, as described by Weimer (2002), are that it

- Focuses attention squarely on the learning process
- Focuses on what the student is learning, how the student is learning, the conditions under which the student is learning, and whether the student is retaining and applying the learning
- Focuses on how current learning positions the student for future learning
- Focuses on learning, not grades
- Empowers learners to take on the learning task
- Gives learners input into the assessment process
- Ensures that the instructor retains responsibility for monitoring progress and assigning the final grade, if one is necessary

We review these and other means by which assessment of this nature can be performed in the online environment in Part Two of this book. Grading becomes easier when learners are involved in the learning and assessment process, as self-assessment becomes a critical component.

## Student Involvement and the Element of Choice

McVay Lynch (2002) notes that learners should be involved in the development of the assessment process online. This can also be said of the face-to-face environment. To do so, however, the instructor must be willing to give up control and must believe that the course that he or she has created has already provided the knowledge base that the student needs to gain mastery in the particular content area. McVay Lynch states that when the instructor gives up control and engages the student in the process by using criteria for assessment, the following can result:

- The student is given responsibility for learning and evaluation.
- The student learns to use resources outside of the teacher for ongoing assessment after the course.
- The evaluation reflects a real-world environment instead of that in the classroom.
- The student must use higher-order thinking skills of application, analysis, synthesis, and evaluation in writing a reflection of the event. (p. 125)

A learner-focused assessment designed with student input, such as that which McVay Lynch describes, can apply as much to exams as to other means of student assessment in a course. For example, students might be asked to submit an exam question that would be incorporated into the final exam or to create their own essay question that is approved by the instructor and then answered by the student. Unfortunately, instructors tend to rely on test banks to create exams and use tests and quizzes as their only means of assessing student performance.

Another means by which to involve students in designing assessments is to allow a team or small group to determine what they will submit to the instructor to demonstrate team competence at the close of a collaborative activity. In the case of a presentation to the larger group, for example, the students can be left to determine not only what they will present and how they will present it but also the deliverable that accompanies that presentation. Allowing the students the flexibility to produce a presentation, a web page, a joint paper, a handbook, a brochure, or some other artifact that represents their collaborative learning allows them, as Angelo and Cross (1993) contend, to increase their grasp of course concepts. It is also an important aspect in building an effective learning community. Stein and Wanstreet (2003) note that the element of choice in assessments appears to be a factor critical to learning success with adult learners and that the ability to choose allows students to work from a preferred learning style.

Allowing students to choose, however, does not always go smoothly. Consider a graduate-level course that one of us was teaching. Students were given a collaborative assignment at the beginning of the course to develop a handbook that was due toward the end of the course. Although the general parameters of the assignment were given, it was up to the students to choose what the final product would include. They were also advised to break up into two small groups; the groupings could be based on common interests or a desire to work toward a particular type of handbook. This assignment and the parameters accompanying it had been given to other classes in the same manner, and the students were able to self-organize with little difficulty. This group, however, struggled. Early in the course, one student suggested they begin discussing how they might work together. This was met with a positive response from a number of group members; however, three or four students claimed to have missed this discussion thread and did not participate. About three or four weeks into this twelve-week course, another student became anxious about the lack of progress and called for a division of the large group into two smaller groups. She created the two groups and then proceeded to organize her small group to begin the work on the project, although not all voices had been heard. Another student objected, and conflict resulted. The instructor in this case intervened and set limits around the decision-making process, imposing a time limit of three days during which the group had to make the decisions about how they would proceed. Yet another student stepped forward and negotiated an amicable division of the group into two smaller groups based on the desired content of the handbooks put forth by the group members. In this situation, although time was wasted in negotiation with one another, the groups felt that they learned a tremendous amount about what is necessary for online collaboration and working on a team—both of which were desired outcomes of the course. In cases like this one, instructors may need to set firmer limits or reduce the number of choices available so that students can complete the assignment and the final product can be assessed.

## Aligning Assessment with Course Activities

In many instances the assessment of an online course is not in alignment with the type of instruction that may have occurred in the course. Several years ago we were asked to teach two different online courses at a university—one in social psychology and one a capstone course for a management degree. Both courses were designed using a combination of discussions and authentic activities that encouraged students to bring in real-life examples related to concepts in the course. However, at the end of the term, a multiple-choice and true/false exam was mandated by the program administrators. As instructors, we were not permitted to write the exam—it was written by a department chair—and students were required to take the exam at a proctored site. Every student in both courses failed the exam. The issue was a lack of alignment between the teaching methods used in the course, which were based on the engaged critical model, and a final exam that was based on the transmission model. Students were used to engaging in dialogue and completing assignments that emerged from the lower levels of the learning pyramid. The exam, however, was based on rote memorization of minute facts contained in the textbook. Clearly, this lack of alignment resulted in unhappy students and two unhappy instructors.

McVay Lynch notes that good assessment uses multiple measures of student performance. When instructors use multiple measures and authentic assessments that are based in real life and not just classroom learning, there is more likelihood of alignment with outcomes and competencies, a lower possibility that cheating will occur (a topic we will discuss in more depth in Chapter Two), and an increased likelihood that a true measurement of student competency and performance will result. The use of multiple measures of assessment is simply good pedagogy.

Although we have been focusing on assessment as it pertains to any environment, as we turn now to the application of assessment practices online, we find that many of the same principles apply. Given that a well-designed online course should be learner focused and centered, it follows that student assessment within that course should be the same. The reflective process that should be included in an online course provides the basis for learner-centered assessment. Students should be given credit for self-reflection, and it should be incorporated into the design and expectations for the online course. Each collaborative activity should contain a reflective component. At the very least, students should be asked to reflect on their participation in the activity and their contributions to the group.

In addition, asking students to reflect on the process not only helps enable them to evaluate the activity but also gives the instructor very important formative and summative information that can be incorporated into future iterations of the assignment. We will discuss all of these elements in more depth in the next chapter. Learner-focused assessment, then, can help move students from basic knowledge acquisition and repetition to development as reflective practitioners.

## APPLYING WHAT WE HAVE LEARNED

This chapter has focused on the basics of good assessment, from the development of program competencies to looking at course outcomes, and mapping those to learning objectives and assignments at the unit level of the course. These principles apply to any course, whether it is delivered online or face-to-face, or in a hybrid of the two delivery methods. In the next chapter, we look specifically at the online environment and discuss how these practices translate into good assessment when the major portion of the course is delivered online.

The following key principles were presented in this chapter:

- When designing a course, attention needs to be paid to the alignment of competencies at the program level with outcomes at the course level and with learning objectives at the unit level.
- Assessments should be designed with the end in mind—that is, both competencies and outcomes—and should answer the question, "What is it we want our students to be able to *know and do* at the conclusion of this course?"
- Competencies, outcomes, objectives, and assessments should be learner-focused.
- Assignments should have explicit, clear directions, and grading criteria for the assignment should be equally clear and explicit.

# Assessment Online

chapter TWO

In our discussion to this point, it has become apparent that good course design that aligns competencies with outcomes is critical. This, coupled with assignments and assessments that are varied and also in alignment with course outcomes, leads to a higher level of student performance and satisfaction with the learning process, regardless of the delivery mechanism of the course (Buzzetto-More & Alade, 2006; Lynch, Goold, & Blain, 2004). This can be deemed the basis for best practices in assessment. However, as we have also discussed, online teaching and learning involve different approaches, and thus approaches to assignments and assessments also need to be different. A further complicating factor is that today's college student is used to using the online environment in ways that depart from those involved in the usual and customary ways in which online courses are delivered. Involvement in social networking is different from participating in an online course. The new uses of, and technologies found on, the web can be used to assessment advantage, however. We now turn our attention to the ways in which the online environment changes our approach to assessment and how it may be used to support and assist with the assessment process. This chapter will also address the following questions:

- How do we empower learners to take responsibility for their learning in the online environment through good assessment?
- How can we bring the "real world" into the assessment of online learning?
- How can we incorporate higher-order thinking skills and reflection into online assessments?
- How can good online assessment practice help move students from basic knowledge acquisition and repetition to development as reflective practitioners?

## PRINCIPLES OF EFFECTIVE ONLINE ASSESSMENT

Angelo and Cross (1993) support the notion that for assessment to be effective, it must be embedded in and aligned with the design of the course. They note a number of characteristics of effective classroom assessment: it is learner-centered, teacher-directed, mutually beneficial, formative, context-specific, ongoing, and firmly rooted in good practice. Although they are discussing assessment techniques for the face-to-face classroom, these same principles can be effectively applied to the online classroom. How, then, do these principles change when we move online?

The following are some principles that should guide student assessment in an online course:

- Design learner-centered assessments that include self-reflection.
- Design and include grading rubrics for the assessment of contributions to the discussion as well as for assignments, projects, and collaboration itself.
- Include collaborative assessments through public posting of papers, along with comments from student to student.
- Encourage students to develop skills in providing feedback by providing guidelines to good feedback and by modeling what is expected.
- Use assessment techniques that fit the context and align with learning objectives.
- Design assessments that are clear, easy to understand, and likely to work in the online environment.
- Ask for and incorporate student input into how assessment should be conducted. (Palloff & Pratt, 2003, pp. 101–102)

We will now explore each of these principles individually.

## Design Learner-Centered Assessments That Include Self-Reflection

Given that a well-designed online course should be learner focused and centered, it follows that student assessment within that course should be the same. As we noted previously, Weimer (2002) describes a key characteristic of learner-focused teaching as focusing attention squarely on the learning process. When the learning process changes, the assessment process should change with it. Additionally, Weimer notes the importance of empowering learners in both the learning and assessment processes. In the online environment, empowerment takes the form of student responsibility for learning activities, such as (1) discussions, (2) participation in collaborative activities, and (3) self-reflection as an important mode of assessment.

The reflective process that should be included in an online course actually provides a foundation for learner-centered assessment. Students should be given credit for self-reflection, and it should be incorporated into the design and expectations for the online course. Students should be asked to reflect on their progress at least twice during the course—at midterm and at the end. A popular assignment suggested by Angelo and Cross (1993), which can also be used for self-assessment purposes, is the One-Minute Paper. In a face-to-face class, the instructor might take the last few minutes of class time to ask students to reflect on and answer the following two questions:

- What was the most important thing you learned in this class?
- What questions remain unanswered?

In an online class, these questions might be assigned at the close of each week's discussion or at the end of each unit. One of us uses this approach weekly and augments it by also asking, "What did you contribute to the learning process this week?"

Another means by which ongoing self-assessment can be achieved is through the use of Stephen Brookfield's (1995) Critical Incident Questionnaire (CIQ). A form of ongoing formative assessment, the CIQ consists of five questions and is designed to be used at the close of a face-to-face class. It can, however, be adapted to the online environment in a similar fashion to the One-Minute Paper and can be extremely useful not only as a self-assessment tool but also for receiving ongoing information about what is working or not working in the online class. Here are the CIQ questions:

1. At what moment in class this week did you feel most engaged with what was happening?
2. At what moment in the class this week did you feel most distanced from what was happening?
3. What action that anyone (teacher or student) took in class this week did you find most affirming and helpful?
4. What action that anyone (teacher or student) took in class this week did you find most puzzling or confusing?
5. What about the class this week surprised you the most? (This could be about your own reactions to what went on, or something that someone did, or anything else that concerns you.)

Yet another means by which self-assessment and formative assessment can be linked is through the use of web-based tools, such as the Student Assessment of Learning Gains (SALG). Designed predominantly by science instructors at the University of Wisconsin who were concerned about assessing how well students understood and were integrating material presented in a course, the site can now be used by instructors from any discipline interested in knowing how well course elements are promoting learning. Items can be modified to fit the content of a course, and reports can be generated that promote formative assessment of the learning process while generating self-assessment data for students.

Rubrics, which we will discuss in more detail later, can form a basis for self-reflection by defining and delineating performance expectations in such a way that learners can look at the categories of performance, reflect on their own contributions to the course, and determine where they fall on the grid. They can then send a copy of the rubric to the instructor with elements highlighted or underlined that indicate self-reflection on performance, with comments added. This opens the door to dialogue with the instructor regarding learner performance. Even the hard sciences and mathematics courses can use this approach to help learners determine what has been mastered and what is yet to be learned in the online course.

Each collaborative activity embedded in an online course should contain a reflective component. At the very least, students should be asked to reflect on their participation in the activity and their contributions to the group. In addition, asking students to reflect on the process not only allows them to evaluate the activity but also gives the instructor very important formative and summative information that can be incorporated into future iterations of the assignment.

### Design and Include Grading Rubrics

This section addresses the principle of designing and including grading rubrics for the assessment of contributions to the discussion and for assignments, projects, and collaboration itself. A study conducted by Gaytan and McEwan (2007) found that both students and instructors value the use of rubrics as a means of assessment and as a way of providing meaningful and rapid feedback to learners. Rubrics help to define the characteristics of a high-quality assignment and help the student understand assignment and assessment expectations. Rubrics also provide a range of performance by establishing categories that span the range of possible outcomes, from basic to exceptional performance on a task. Conrad and Donaldson (2004) describe a rubric as a tool that "defines the performance levels for each gradable activity element" (p. 26). As such, rubrics provide students with a concrete way of evaluating their own performance as well as the performance of the members of their team in collaborative work. Having a well-developed rubric assists the instructor with the "How am I doing?" questions that often emerge in an online course. The use of rubrics helps to take the guesswork out of grading. This not only provides a realistic picture of how a student interacted with course material and their peers but also reduces the possibilities of grade inflation, dissatisfaction, and grade appeals by providing evaluative material that is more objective and quantifiable. Points can be assigned to each category of performance, making the conversion from points to grade a much easier task. In Part Two we will go into detail about rubric development, and in the Additional Resources section we offer resources and websites that facilitate rubric construction.

Rubrics can also be used, as we've previously discussed, as a basis for self-reflection, allowing students to compare their own performance with the performance expectations defined in each category. Exhibit 2.1 presents an example of a rubric used to assess discussion in an online course. The first example shows the rubric as posted in the course. The second example shows an annotated rubric submitted by a student for self-assessment purposes, with the student's

## Exhibit 2.1
## Rubric for Participation in Discussions: Example 1

| Criteria | Nonperformance (0 points) | Basic (1 point) | Proficient (2 points) | Distinguished (3 points) |
|---|---|---|---|---|
| **Includes and applies relevant course concepts, theories, or materials correctly with citation of sources.** | Does not explain relevant course concepts, theories, or materials. Does not provide citation of sources. | Summarizes relevant course concepts, theories, or materials. Provides citation some of the time. | Applies and analyzes relevant course concepts, theories, or materials correctly. Provides citation most of the time. | Evaluates and synthesizes course concepts, theories, or materials correctly, using examples or supporting evidence. Consistently provides citation. |
| **Responds to fellow learners, relating the discussion to relevant course concepts and providing substantive feedback.** | Does not respond to fellow learners. | Responds to fellow learners without relating discussion to the relevant course concepts. Provides feedback, but it is not substantive. | Responds to fellow learners, relating the discussion to relevant course concepts. Feedback is substantive most of the time. | Responds to fellow learners, relating the discussion to relevant course concepts, and consistently extends the dialogue through provision of substantive feedback. |
| **Applies relevant professional, personal, or other real-world experiences.** | Does not contribute professional, personal, or other real-world experiences. | Contributes some professional, personal, or other real-world experiences that may or may not relate to course content. | Applies relevant professional, personal, or other real-world experiences. | Applies relevant professional, personal, or other real-world experiences and extends the dialogue by responding to the examples of peers. |
| **Supports position with applicable resources beyond assigned reading.** | Does not establish relevant position. | Establishes relevant position but does minimal outside research. | Consistently supports position with additional resources. | Validates position with applicable resources and supports the learning of others through the contribution of additional resources. |

### Rubric for Participation in Discussions: Example 2

| Criteria | Nonperformance (0 points) | Basic (1 point) | Proficient (2 points) | Distinguished (3 points) | Comments |
|---|---|---|---|---|---|
| **Includes and applies relevant course concepts, theories, or materials correctly with citation of sources.** | Does not explain relevant course concepts, theories, or materials. Does not provide citation of sources. | Summarizes relevant course concepts, theories, or materials. Provides citation some of the time. | ***Applies and analyzes relevant course concepts, theories, or materials correctly. Provides citation most of the time.*** | Evaluates and synthesizes course concepts, theories, or materials correctly, using examples or supporting evidence. Consistently provides citation. | *I've been keeping up with the reading but I haven't been using citations in my postings consistently.* |
| **Responds to fellow learners, relating the discussion to relevant course concepts and providing substantive feedback.** | Does not respond to fellow learners. | Responds to fellow learners without relating discussion to the relevant course concepts. Provides feedback, but it is not substantive. | Responds to fellow learners, relating the discussion to relevant course concepts. Feedback is substantive most of the time. | ***Responds to fellow learners, relating the discussion to relevant course concepts, and consistently extends the dialogue through provision of substantive feedback.*** | *I think I've done a really good job of responding to my peers and to being actively involved in discussion.* |
| **Applies relevant professional, personal, or other real-world experiences.** | Does not contribute professional, personal, or other real-world experiences. | Contributes some professional, personal, or other real-world experiences that may or may not relate to course content. | Applies relevant professional, personal, or other real-world experiences. | ***Applies relevant professional, personal, or other real-world experiences and extends the dialogue by responding to the examples of peers.*** | *I always bring in examples from my work and my life to extend discussion. I've also been commenting on the examples my peers have provided.* |
| **Supports position with applicable resources beyond assigned reading.** | Does not establish relevant position. | ***Establishes relevant position but does minimal outside research.*** | Consistently supports position with additional resources. | Validates position with applicable resources and supports the learning of others through the contribution of additional resources. | *This is the area where I've really fallen short. I've only read the textbook and haven't done any outside research. I need to improve this.* |

own performance assessments in boldface italic and italic comments in a right-hand column.

## Include Collaborative Assessments

In this section, we cover the inclusion of collaborative assessments through public posting of papers along with comments from student to student. In our previous work (Palloff & Pratt, 2005, 2007), we have extensively discussed the importance and benefit of collaboration in online courses. Collaborative effort helps learners achieve a deeper level of knowledge generation while moving from independence to interdependence, thus strengthening the foundation of an online learning community, which we believe is the vehicle through which the course should be delivered. Brookfield (1995) contends that collaborative processes promote initiative on the part of the learners, as well as creativity and critical thinking skills. Collaboration also allows for meaningful dialogue, which is clearly critical to the discussion aspects of the online course. By learning together in a learning community, students have the opportunity to extend and deepen their learning experience, test out new ideas by sharing them with a supportive group, and receive critical and constructive feedback. The likelihood of successful achievement of learning objectives in a given unit and in overall course outcomes increases through collaborative engagement.

Although group projects, and particularly the assessment of those projects, can be more challenging in the online environment, establishing guidelines for collaboration and collaborative assessment can help with this task. A simple rule to remember when assessing collaborative work is that collaborative activities are best assessed collaboratively. At the conclusion of a collaborative activity, we generally ask our students to submit a self-assessment of their own contributions to and participation in the activity, along with a peer assessment that does the same for all members of the group. The instructor should certainly retain the determination about what to assess, how to assess it, and how to respond to any evaluation material gathered through the reflective material submitted by students. It is, after all, the instructor's responsibility to record a final grade for the course and to follow up with those who are not performing. However, the information gathered through collaborative assessment should not be given less emphasis than the information gathered through direct observation or evaluation by the instructor. The following questions can be used to guide the self-assessment:

- How well did I participate in my group? Was I a team player?
- Did I make a significant contribution?
- Did I share my portion of the work load?
- How comfortable do I feel with the group process?
- Did I feel comfortable expressing any problems or concerns openly?
- Did I provide substantive feedback to other group members?
- How do I feel about the collaborative work produced by my group?
- How well did the collaborative process contribute to my learning goals and objectives for this course? (Palloff & Pratt, 2007, p. 184)

We further ask students to assign a letter grade to their assessments of themselves and their peers, and we consider the grades very seriously as we conduct our own assessment of the work. Finally, we assign two grades for the assignment—one is a group grade for the final product of the group, the other an individual grade assigned to each member of the group.

The use of peer review (for the purpose of critique) and peer assessment (critique and suggested grade) assists with this function in collaborative activities. Often, in face-to-face classes, time constraints can interfere with effective use of peer assessment. However, in the asynchronous online environment, papers and assignments can be posted for easy viewing by other students (Michigan State University, 2005). Students can be paired in dyads as review partners or put in small groups for this purpose. The peer and self-assessment processes can also be assisted by the use of websites and software tools designed for this purpose. One such site is Calibrated Peer Review (CPR), which allows instructors to use already created writing assignments for assessment purposes or create their own assignments and criteria for peer and self-assessment. The use of websites or tools requires some time to set up, but simplifies the peer assessment task and also provides a more objective assessment. If a website or tool is not used, then guidelines for peer review should be provided to the students. Exhibit 2.2 provides an example of a feedback form that might be provided to students to help guide their process in reviewing a student colleague's paper.

To use feedback forms for peer review effectively, the instructor can provide a sample paper that has been scored using the form. Students can also be given a practice session with instructor feedback about how well they did in their peer review effort. Most important, however, students need to be given

**Exhibit 2.2**
**Sample Feedback Form for Peer Review**

| Criteria | Weak | Satisfactory | Strong | Reader Comments |
|---|---|---|---|---|
| *Clarity*<br>Writing is clear and importance of message comes through. | | | | |
| *Evidence*<br>Supportive research and citations are present. | | | | |
| *Organization*<br>Paper is well organized and ideas flow well from one to the next. Subheads are used effectively. | | | | |
| *Mechanics and APA Style*<br>Contains few or no grammar and mechanical errors and is formatted correctly. | | | | |
| *Effectiveness*<br>The overall product is effective and convincing and shows mastery of the topic. | | | | |

clear information about the expectations for the assignment being completed and for the peer review process, and effective ways to provide feedback, a topic we will now discuss.

## Encourage Students to Develop Good Feedback Skills

We can encourage students to develop their skills in providing good feedback by giving them guidelines to how this is done and by modeling what is expected. Conrad and Donaldson (2004) note, "In an engaged learning environment, peers often have the best perspective on whether their teammates are providing valuable contributions to the learning community. Therefore, learning environments that encourage collaborative activities should incorporate peer evaluations in the assessment process. . . . The key to effective peer feedback is that it be constructive and encourage improvement" (p. 27). Activities that involve peer feedback can include responses to discussion questions, peer review of papers and projects, and fishbowl activities—wherein one or more students participate in an activity "in the bowl" (that is, in a designated discussion forum in which only a small group of students work together) while others observe and provide feedback. Students don't necessarily just *know* how to provide good feedback. Consequently, it is important for the instructor to provide guidelines to students that support them in developing this skill. We offer sample guidelines for effective feedback in Part Two. Encouraging their use can help to alleviate the problems and concerns involved with using student feedback as an assessment tool.

Additionally, rubrics that include points for providing effective feedback are likely to encourage students to use the guidelines in constructing feedback and to be more honest and constructive in the feedback they deliver to one another. Communication guidelines that include the use of good "netiquette" and professional communication should be established at the start of any course. Students should then be encouraged to maintain professional communication with one another at all times and should not assume that the friendly relationships they have had in working with one another will cure all ills should someone stumble into what might be considered inappropriate communication.

Finally, the instructor needs to act as a model of good feedback. The tone, frequency, and mode of delivery of feedback will be picked up by students and followed. One of us taught a course in which drafts of final papers were posted on the discussion board for peer feedback. The instructor also posted feedback to each paper using the Track Changes feature in Word and was very careful to keep the feedback supportive, neutral, and professional. Very shortly thereafter, the learners also began using Track Changes with one another, and in their final reflections for the course they commented about how helpful this was to them. Through modeling, they were taught a new skill that they could then transfer into other assessment activities in other courses.

## Use Effective Assessment Techniques

In Chapter One we devoted considerable attention to the use of assessment techniques that fit the context and align with learning objectives. However, we did not discuss specific assessment techniques that promote alignment. We noted that Morgan and O'Reilly (1999) believe that if an online course is designed with clear guidelines and objectives and with tasks and assignments that are relevant not only to the subject matter but to students' lives as well, and if students understand what is expected of them, assessment will be in alignment with the course as a whole and will not be seen as a separate and cumbersome task. Keeping this principle in mind should also promote the use of assessments that move beyond tests, quizzes, and other exercises in rote memorization. Although tests and quizzes are useful in assessing some aspects of online work, they should not be the main means of assessment. Keep in mind that *a variety of assessment techniques should be employed to effectively assess student performance online*. This is also in keeping with our simple rule: the collaborative activity embedded in an online course, be it a discussion activity or group project, is best assessed by collaborative means. For example, in a mathematics class, the instructor may set up collaborative homework forums and group problem-solving activities, but may still use tests and quizzes to assess individual acquisition of skills. An accounting professor might set up an authentic assessment using a simulated business organization and ask students to set up accounting systems for the organization, while, again, using tests and quizzes to determine whether individual students understand the accounting principles involved. This grouping of assessment activities would be in alignment with course objectives, the subject matter being studied, and the need to determine competency or skill acquisition.

However, many online instructors have noted the difficulty of using tests and quizzes as effective assessments of student learning. Many feel that more authentic assessments—such as projects, papers, and artifacts that integrate course concepts—are more effective means by which to assess student learning online. Therefore, the use of self-reflections, peer assessments, and clearly designed rubrics designating good projects and papers may align more closely with the objectives of an online course and flow more easily into course content.

## Designing Effective Assessments for the Online Environment

How can we design assessments that are clear, easy to understand, and likely to work in the online environment? Gaytan (2005) suggests a number of effective techniques that can be used to create assessments that work well in the online environment, including the following:

- The provision of regular, ongoing communication with and feedback to students as a means by which to embed assessment in the course itself

- The inclusion of dynamic interaction, defined by the use of group work, collaboration, and a high level of interaction through discussion
- The modification of traditional assessment tools, such as essays, discussion question responses, and projects that require demonstration of skill acquisition and problem-solving ability
- The use of alternative assessments, such as performance-based assessments, authentic assessments, and the use of e-portfolios

Rasmussen and Northrup (1999) provide indicators for the use of each of these forms of assessment. We have augmented their indicators with examples of activities for each and will provide detailed descriptions of these forms of assessment in Part Two.

- *Performance assessments.* These allow the instructor to observe students applying skills in action. The end result is a product developed by the learners. *Fishbowl activities and wikis, or socially constructed web pages, are good means through which this can be accomplished.*
- *Authentic assessments.* These allow students to work under the same conditions and use the same materials as they might in a real-world environment. *Simulation activities and the use of real-world case studies are means by which authentic assessments can be carried out.*
- *Portfolio assessments.* These allow students to demonstrate progress over time through the showcasing of papers, projects, homework, journal or blog entries, and the like, which are stored electronically. *Presentations or demonstrations of accumulated learning can accompany the e-portfolio, and review can occur in discussion with the instructor, with a resulting joint assessment of progress or overall learning.*

A discussion of assessment techniques that work well online would not be complete without covering the effective use of tests and quizzes. It has been noted that the use of practice exams and self-quizzes based on homework align well with courses that use exams for grading, as students develop understanding of what will be expected in terms of types of questions and how to use the technology for the test (Michigan State University, 2005). Concern about potential cheating on online exams has promoted the practice of using proctored exams. Generally, these are set up by asking students at a distance to find a proctored site or by asking groups of students to come to campus to take the final exam. However, both approaches can prove cumbersome and inconvenient for both instructors and students, and the use of proctors is not foolproof. Most course management systems allow for the randomization of test questions so that, in essence, each student receives an individual exam, reducing the possibility of cheating. Michigan State University reports that in an online remedial math course offered jointly by Michigan State and San Francisco State Universities, students were given five randomized online exams and two in-person proctored exams. The math faculty at SFSU compared the results of both types of exams and found a high level of consistency in the grades, suggesting that cheating did not occur and that the randomization of exam items provides some measure of confidence.

Major and Taylor (2003) note that online exams should be viewed as take-home exams, as students will likely use books and notes to complete the exam. They further assert that when students enter the workforce, they will not be asked to solve problems from memory or without using reference materials. Consequently, establishing a testing situation that simulates the real-life use of the information can create a form of authentic assessment.

### Ask for and Incorporate Student Input

It is helpful to ask students for their input on how assessment should be conducted and then incorporate it into assessment design. Angelo and Cross (1993) state, "By cooperating in assessment, students reinforce their grasp of the course content and strengthen their own skills at self-assessment" (pp. 4–5). Bachman (2000) notes that the focus on learner-centered teaching has led to greater involvement of learners in directing their own assessment process through asking them to determine how they want to be assessed and through the use of self-assessment tools. The practices of constructivism (Brooks & Brooks, 1993; Cranton, 1994; Jonassen, Davidson, Collins, Campbell, & Haag, 1995) and active learning (Myers & Jones, 1993) suggest that learners actively create knowledge and meaning through experimentation, exploration, and the manipulation and testing of ideas in reality. In a constructivist classroom, it is the interaction and feedback from others that assist in determining the accuracy and application of ideas. Involving students in the development of assessments helps to move a learner from the role of student to that of reflective practitioner. Sparked by reflective questions, collaboration, feedback, and the linking of learning to experience, students begin to reflect on their learning process, thus transforming how they perceive themselves as learners.

Other contributions to adult learning theory (Knowles, 1973, 1990; Hase & Kenyon, 2000) have supported the importance of self-direction for learning. Although some may argue that traditional undergraduates lack the ability to be self-directed, we assert that through the development of learning activities that promote self-direction—such as collaborative assignments and self-assessments—learners can be taught the skills that will move them toward greater ability to be involved in the development of assessments in the online classroom. Asking learners to become involved in the development of the assessment process, then, creates a cycle of learning that supports their growth as learners. Instructors should involve learners in assessment design when the desired outcomes are

- An increased sense of community
- Promotion of self-directed learning, self-efficacy, and discovery
- Increased problem-solving skills
- Introduction of the element of choice in assessment

Involvement of learners in the assessment process is based on the beliefs that students can be the experts when it comes to their own learning and that the promotion of self-direction is important.

## ASSESSMENT AND THE ONLINE LEARNER

Morgan and O'Reilly (1999) offer six key qualities for assessment of online students:

- A clear rationale and consistent pedagogical approach
- Explicit values, aims, criteria, and standards
- Authentic and holistic tasks
- A facilitative degree of structure
- Sufficient and timely formative assessment
- Awareness of the learning context and perceptions

According to Morgan and O'Reilly, assessments should be both (1) formative, meaning that they occur throughout the course and inform practice, and (2) summative, meaning that they occur at the end of the course and assess cumulative learning from the course. In the next chapter, we will focus on effective means of completing course evaluations that are based on the concepts we have been presenting thus far—in other words, course evaluations that align with the outcomes set forth for the course and the competencies that learners can hope to achieve by the end of their program of study.

Clear differences exist between classroom assessment and online assessment, and these differences should be obvious to the learner. As we have noted, replicating assessments that are used in the face-to-face classroom without modification for online use is likely to cause frustration for learners. Regardless of setting, however, good assessment can reduce the gap between what was taught and what was learned. Speck (2002) discusses the differences between the traditional and alternative paradigms in assessment. The traditional method is based on the scientific method and is generally represented by the use of exams. As we have noted, however—and Speck supports this—the use of exams online creates issues of security and limits professional judgment in assessment of student performance. He notes that the traditional approach promotes rote exercises that offer limited insight into student ability. The alternative paradigm is social in nature, views learning as a process, and gives students the opportunity to explore concepts together and to make mistakes.

Byers (2002) notes that the learner-centered paradigm holds the implication that students themselves are the primary learning resource. Clearly, involvement in collaborative activity in an online course creates a learner-centered focus that calls for learner-centered assessment, meaning that the student becomes the main resource for and source of assessment information. The more we engage our students in a process of ongoing assessment of their own performance, the more meaningful the online course will be to them.

## USING THE ONLINE ENVIRONMENT FOR ASSESSMENT ADVANTAGE

Many of today's students are entering online classrooms with a higher level of technical skill than their instructors possess. Younger students are actively engaged in the use of applications that promote social networking and the ability to exercise control over the use of one's own data in terms of what is posted and maintained on such sites as MySpace or Friendster. These sites also allow for direct access to the person who has posted the material and promote the establishment of an online presence through profiles, blogs, links to videos and music, and so on.

Some instructors are becoming acquainted with these technologies in order to better use them in the development of their online courses and the assessment of online learners. The online environment and what is known as "Web 2.0" applications can also be used for assessment advantage. The following are some possibilities that we will further discuss in Part Two:

- *Computer-generated and -scored tests and quizzes.* In addition to the ability to develop randomized tests, many course management systems allow for the computer scoring of tests and quizzes as a means of providing immediate feedback to learners. Explanations of incorrect answers can accompany the responses, along with suggestions for what material should be reviewed.
- *Internet-based research projects.* The Internet provides a vast array of possibilities for research. By not only encouraging students to seek out and post what they find to the course but also asking them to critically evaluate the postings of their peers, we can create research activities that also promote the development of critical thinking skills.
- *Peer review and assessment technologies.* The use of such sites and software as Calibrated Peer Review (CPR) and Student Assessment of Learning Gains (SALG) supports the task of peer review, teaches students important skills in reviewing, and also helps to create consistency and objectivity.
- *Internet-based case studies.* Many sites offer case studies for student and instructor use that can form the basis for authentic assessments.
- *WebQuests.* Developed and offered through San Diego State University, WebQuests provide fun internet-based scavenger hunts that can be conducted in teams or individually. Assessment rubrics are built into the activity and become an important component of their use.
- *Synchronous and asynchronous technologies to facilitate collaboration.* The use of blogs, wikis, and virtual classroom technologies promotes collaboration while providing new means for assessment. Journaling through blogs can demonstrate how learners are integrating and applying their thinking around course concepts. Wikis allow students to work together to make meaning of course concepts. Virtual classroom spaces allow students to brainstorm, share documents, and discuss concepts in real time.

The possibilities presented here represent only a small amount of what is possible when instructors make use of the online environment to create course activities and assessments. Using the environment in which the course is delivered helps open the door to many new ideas for assessment that will likely align with course outcomes in unique and innovative ways.

## PLAGIARISM AND CHEATING

The topic of online assessment includes concerns about plagiarism and cheating. We have already noted that the use of randomization in tests and quizzes as well as designing exams as open-book, take-home exams can help to reduce concerns about cheating when tests and quizzes are employed for assessment purposes online. However, other concerns arise, including how we know that the student participating in the assessment is the one taking the course, how to deal with plagiarism, and whether the student actually wrote the paper he or she turned in for the course.

The Illinois Online Network (n.d.) suggests that although a student may be able to get someone to help him or her with one assessment by taking the test in the enrolled student's stead, getting such help throughout an entire course or program is unlikely. They suggest that this likelihood can be avoided by having several short assessments embedded in the activities of the online course.

Many of the strategies we have suggested for assessment in online courses—providing varied and multiple means of assessment—have the added benefit of reducing the likelihood or possibility of cheating. Additionally, the use of performance-based or authentic assessments reduces the possibility of plagiarism; when writing assignments are related to real-life situations known only to the learner, it is difficult to plagiarize or purchase a paper from a paper mill. Also, asking students to submit sections of the work as it is developed, rather than waiting until the end, can help to detect plagiarism early and can even provide an opportunity through which the student can be educated about appropriate use of sources. McNett (2002) suggests that "deadline-driven desperation" is a common and significant reason for plagiarism and cheating. When we ask students to submit components of a paper throughout the term, not only are students better able to manage their time on a final project, but this also allows the instructor to become more familiar with the student's writing style. Any sudden changes would become a red flag for potential plagiarism, allowing the instructor to intervene.

Varvel (2005) offers some tips for spotting papers that might have been produced by another student or purchased from a paper mill. First, he suggests that copied or purchased papers rarely have quotes. This may be due to poor citation skills or because the use of citations can be a trigger if search engines are being used to track plagiarism. Another hint is the inclusion of old or anachronistic material. One of us received a paper on current approaches to addiction treatment that contained citations that were approximately twenty years old. A plagiarism detection software program flagged the paper as a purchased paper. Finally, Varvel suggests that a student may use topic diversion—in other words, at the end of the term, the student may turn in a paper that is close to but not exactly what the assignment called for. This may be an indicator that the student used an old paper or found one that was close enough to avoid detection. Asking students to submit pieces of the paper (such as a topic statement, annotated reference list, and an outline) or early drafts, assigning topics that require students to apply the material to their lives or work, requiring analysis and synthesis as part of the assignment, and requiring the incorporation of unique resources all can help to deter plagiarism, the use of purchased papers, and the reuse of old papers.

Plagiarism occurs in both face-to-face and online classes. Some believe this is due to a belief that cheating is now considered socially acceptable behavior (Rowe, 2004; Varvel, 2005). Surveys conducted at numerous universities around the country indicate that plagiarism occurs regularly in both face-to-face and online classes and the majority of students know another student who has plagiarized an assignment. The majority believe that the plagiarism was accidental and due to the lack of knowledge about how to properly cite sources. Consequently, a course that is designed with information or links to information about how source material is appropriately used can help. Many institutions use plagiarism detection software, such as Turnitin, My Drop Box, Plagiarism.com, or EVE2. Rather than using the tools punitively, having students run their own work through the software and then using the report generated as a teaching tool help maintain a learner-centered focus while teaching students about paraphrasing and proper use of references.

## APPLYING WHAT WE HAVE LEARNED

In this chapter we have discussed the ways in which assessment changes when we move online. Additionally, we looked at what constitutes best practices in online assessment and the various activities that can be incorporated into an assessment scheme for an online class. In Part Two of this book, we will discuss each of these in detail and offer suggestions for their development and use. In the next chapter, we will turn to the important topic of course and program evaluation, using the same learner-focused, competency-based approach we have been promoting.

The following are the key principles in online assessment presented in this chapter:

- Design learner-centered assessments that align with learner-centered activities and assignments.
- Construct courses that contain a variety of learning activities and assessment measures that tap various learning styles and inhibit the possibilities for plagiarism and cheating.
- Promote, use, and assess learner contributions to the discussion board.
- Use rubrics that establish performance expectations and provide a sound basis for self-assessment.
- Provide prompt feedback on assessments and assignments.
- Consider tests and quizzes delivered online to be "open book" measures and develop them with this factor in mind.
- To make online assessments effective, include performance assessment, authentic assessment, projects, portfolios, self-assessments, peer assessments, and weekly assignments that include discussion assignments.

chapter
THREE

# Course and Program Evaluation

Up to this point we have been focusing on assessment of individual student performance within an online course. However, as we discussed in our review of assessment basics, there need to be strong links among assessment of student performance at the course outcome level, the competencies developed for the online program of study, and the mission of the university to create alignment. Effective course and program evaluation, then, needs to be based on many of the same principles we have been presenting for student assessment. We now turn our attention to ways in which this can be accomplished.

## COURSE EVALUATION

Roberts, Irani, Telg, and Lundy (2005) note that most courses in higher education institutions are evaluated by surveying student attitudes and reactions toward the course at its conclusion. With online courses, additional questions might be asked regarding the technology in use and the instructional strategies employed to promote interaction between the student and instructor. They note the need to create evaluation instruments that respond to the ways in which instruction occurs online, but then go on to suggest the use of an instrument that focuses only on the performance of the instructor in the online environment. Brookfield (1995) states that traditional course evaluations rarely measure what we want them to measure. He describes course evaluations as a popularity contest, as they generally ask students to rate how much they liked or disliked the instructor.

In the learner-focused online classroom, course evaluations should focus not on whether or not the student liked the instructor but on whether the course provided an opportunity for learning. Angelo and Cross (1993) suggest that instructors ask themselves three questions when evaluating their own courses: What are the essential skills and knowledge I am trying to teach? How can I find out whether students are learning them? How can I help students learn better? Responses to these questions point directly to the outcomes developed for the course and look at how successful the course activities were in helping students master them. When the focus is on formative as well as summative evaluation, instructors can receive ongoing answers to these questions as the course is in session and can adjust as necessary to ensure outcome achievement, rather than finding out at the end that activities were not as successful as hoped.

Given, however, that most institutions require some form of summative course evaluation at the conclusion of the term, it is important to create an evaluation that reflects the interactive, more self-directed and learner-focused nature of online learning. Arbaugh (2000) suggests that there are four general categories of factors that influence online learning and should be incorporated into evaluation of online courses: perceived usefulness and ease of the course, flexibility for students and instructors, ease of and emphasis on interaction, and experiences with engagement. Consequently, using these categories as a foundation, a summative evaluation for an online course should contain the following elements:

- Perception of the overall online course experience
- Orientation to the course and course materials
- The content—including the quantity and quality of material presented
- Discussion and interaction with other students and the instructor
- Self-assessment of the level of participation and performance in the course as well as the degree of contribution to the learning of others
- The course management system—ease of use and ability to support learning in the course

- Technical support
- Access to resources

In Part Two, we offer a sample course evaluation that we have used for our own courses in conjunction with a self-assessment that incorporates these elements.

## INSTRUCTOR EVALUATION

As institutions implement online distance learning programs, they are faced with two important tasks: training and development for online instructors and determining effective means by which to evaluate their performance. As already noted, asking students to reflect on instructor performance is one source of evaluative material. However, given the number of factors influencing student satisfaction with a course—the technology in use, ease of access to materials, the ability to interact easily with peers as well as the instructor, and so on—simply asking students how well the instructor performed or whether the instructor was present and provided help on course activities does not provide an adequate basis for evaluation.

Williams (2003) suggests that significant research needs to be conducted on instructor roles and competencies so as to adequately train and evaluate online instructors. His research reveals that the most important competencies for online instructors are instructional designer, instructor or facilitator, trainer (including training students to use the technology, modeling the use of internet technologies, and acting as an advisor), and leader or change agent (described as the modeling of behavior and skills and command of general education theory). In our own experience of training online instructors through our Teaching in the Virtual Classroom program, we have found that online instructors believe that instructional design and course facilitation skills are the most important to successful course delivery. It is important to remember, however, that many instructors do not write or design the courses they teach. Clearly, in these cases, the focus of evaluation should be on course delivery and facilitation for successful learning outcomes.

### Administrative Reviews

Another concern regarding faculty evaluation is who conducts the review. Tobin (2004) points out that many administrators who are called on to evaluate online instructors have never taught online themselves. Consequently, the evaluation tends to be based on criteria that apply to traditional face-to-face delivery and tends to evaluate the wrong things when it comes to teaching online. For example, instructors may be rated on the number of postings they contribute to the discussion board rather than on skills at facilitating student-to-student discussion that promotes a learner focus. Tobin as well as others (Achtemeier, Morris, & Finnegan, 2003; Graham, Cagiltay, Lim, Craner, & Duffy, 2001; Palloff & Pratt, 2003) have suggested a modification of Chickering and Gamson's (1987) *Seven Principles for Good Practice in Undergraduate Education* as a means by which online instructor evaluation can be shaped. The following are the principles with the modifications suggested by Graham et al. for applications to the online course:

Principle 1: Good Practice Encourages Student-Faculty Contact

*Lesson for online instruction:* Instructors should provide clear guidelines for interaction with students.

Principle 2: Good Practice Encourages Cooperation Among Students

*Lesson for online instruction:* Well-designed discussion assignments facilitate meaningful cooperation among students.

Principle 3: Good Practice Encourages Active Learning

*Lesson for online instruction:* Students should present course projects.

Principle 4: Good Practice Gives Prompt Feedback

*Lesson for online instruction:* Instructors need to provide two types of feedback—information feedback and acknowledgment feedback.

Principle 5: Good Practice Emphasizes Time on Task

*Lesson for online instruction:* Online courses need deadlines.

Principle 6: Good Practice Communicates High Expectations

*Lesson for online instruction:* Challenging tasks, sample cases, and praise for quality work communicate high expectations.

Principle 7: Good Practice Respects Diverse Talents and Ways of Working

*Lesson for online instruction:* Allowing students to choose project topics allows diverse views to emerge.

By becoming familiar with the principles of online facilitation, an administrator could develop a checklist that uses the modified seven principles to review an online course and instructor performance within that course.

Sunal, Sunal, Odell, and Sundberg (2003) have developed the Checklist for Online Interactive Learning (COIL); this looks at measurable outcomes of online facilitation, focusing on four areas:

- Student behaviors that meet criterion, such as the demonstration of prerequisite technology skills, the provision of support to and seeking support from peers and instructor, active participation, the use of a variety of communication techniques, and personalizing (that is, establishing social presence)
- Faculty-student interactions, such as the provision of clear guidance, personalized communications, provision of a variety of communication techniques, delineation of institutional policy on academic honesty, maintenance of frequently asked questions, and providing students with continuous and frequent support and feedback
- Provision of technology support by ensuring a low level of technological difficulties and adequate and easy support
- Provision of a learning environment that is equitable, equal access to communications, and use of the discussion board, as well as structured authentic activities, flexible deadlines, social interaction, sequencing of content, a well-organized course site, a welcoming and safe environment, opportunities for collaboration, and ice-breaker activities at the start and reflective activities at the end

Although some of the criteria in the COIL—such as the provision of technical support—may be out of the instructor's hands, many of the criteria listed make up good online facilitation practice as we have discussed it and also support the seven principles for effective teaching for the online classroom. These criteria could be used effectively by administrators who may not have taught online, as they would guide them to look in the right direction for good online teaching practice.

Yet another means by which online courses might be evaluated is the development of a rubric that looks at important elements in course development and delivery. This is particularly useful in evaluating courses that are written and delivered by the same instructor; it can also be applied to just the delivery or facilitation aspects of the course. Roblyer and Wiencke (2003) have proposed just such a rubric of interactivity in an online course. Interactivity is only one of the elements in the COIL, but clearly it is critically important in looking at instructor performance online. The continuum in Exhibit 3.1 illustrates the degrees of interactivity as defined by Roblyer and Wiencke.

In Part Two, we provide a sample checklist we have devised that makes use of the seven principles and critical elements of the COIL for use in faculty evaluation, as well as a modification of Roblyer and Wiencke's rubric for interactivity.

**Exhibit 3.1**
**Continuum of Interactivity**

| Low | Minimum | Moderate | Above Average | High |
|---|---|---|---|---|
| Limited social interaction<br>Brief intros and bios<br>One-way delivery of information<br>Interaction only with instructor<br>Interaction is instructor to student and only when required | Intros and bios used<br>Students communicate with instructor mostly via e-mail<br>Minimal voluntary interaction between students and between instructor and students (<25%) | Intros and bios used<br>Ice-breaker activity used to increase rapport "<br>Use of discussion board"<br>Students required to work together in pairs or small groups<br>Moderate voluntary interaction between students and between instructor and students (25% to 50%) | Intros and bios used<br>Multiple activities designed to increase social rapport<br>Collaborative activity included<br>Use of discussion board<br>Use of teleconferencing<br>Above-average voluntary communication between students and between instructor and students (50% to 75%) | Intros and bios used<br>A variety of activities conducted in class and outside of class to promote rapport<br>Collaborative activities included that also use outside experts<br>Use of discussion board<br>Teleconferencing, video conferencing used<br>High level of voluntary communication between students and between instructor and students (>75%) |

## Peer Review and Mentoring

Yet another effective means by which online faculty evaluation can be accomplished is the use of a peer review and peer mentoring program. Mandernach, Donnelli, Dailey, and Schulte (2005) share the very extensive model used by Park University in Missouri. In this model, all instructors who teach online first go through faculty training for online teaching and then are assigned a peer faculty mentor who monitors their performance in an online course. The courses offered at Park University are eight-week intensive online courses. The mentor conducts five formative reviews of instructor performance:

- A preterm review looks at the way in which the course has been set up.
- A review at the end of week two evaluates the degree to which community building and interactivity have developed.
- A review of the discussion, feedback, and grading occurs at week four.
- At the end of week six, a review of assessment and preparation for final exams occurs.
- During the final weeks of the term, a retrospective review is conducted, looking at overall course climate and organization.

This very intensive mentoring process may not be feasible for many institutions. Consequently, we offer this modified approach to and process for peer review and mentoring:

- Phase 1—*Online Faculty Training.* All new online faculty participate in online training involving not only training on the course management system in use but also best practices in online teaching; community building; effective use of discussions; effective assessments; and university policies governing online courses, grading, and so on. Experienced online faculty participate in a modified version of the training, focusing on university policies and a review of best practices.
- Phase 2—*Shadowing.* Faculty who will be teaching online are assigned to shadow another experienced instructor for a unit or two to see the course in action.
- Phase 3—*Online Teaching with Mentor Shadowing.* Once the instructor has completed shadowing a course and is ready to set up and teach his or her own course, the instructor whose course was shadowed acts as a mentor

and shadows the new instructor's course, offering suggestions as needed. To increase the effectiveness of the mentoring process, the new instructor should designate particular areas in which he or she desires feedback or support. The goal of the evaluation should be continuous quality improvement through identification of strengths and areas that could use additional training and support.

Once a cadre of experienced online faculty have been developed in this way, an ongoing peer review process can be established. DePaul University (2007) has devised such a program of ongoing peer review and provides specific guidelines to reviewers to assist them in preparing a narrative report about what has been observed. The following guidelines, with particular areas of focus, are adapted from the DePaul model:

- *Teaching and learning.* Are the teaching methods used effective in promoting student engagement? Are the materials and the course well organized and presented clearly? Are the reading assignments effective? Is there sufficient rigor?
- *Knowledge of the subject matter.* Does the way the instructor addresses and presents material indicate knowledge of the subject matter? Is presentation coherent, clear, and consistent?
- *Communication.* What types of interactions take place (student-student, student-instructor)? Has the instructor established social presence? Is a learning community present? Is the instructor accessible, respectful, and engaged? Is feedback that is substantive and actionable regularly provided? Is assessment of student work fair? Does the instructor elicit feedback and reflections throughout the course?
- *Enthusiasm.* Does the instructor demonstrate enthusiasm for the topic, for teaching, and for learning?
- *Development of competence.* Does the instructor make implicit and explicit reference to course outcomes and program competencies? Are there clear criteria for assessing how well students have demonstrated competence?

One additional technique for faculty evaluation is the use of portfolios. Just as portfolios work well for assessment of competence for students, they work equally well in the review of faculty performance. Faculty who work at tenure-granting institutions are quite familiar with the preparation of a portfolio of their work and accomplishments. The preparation of a portfolio for online faculty evaluation is not dissimilar, but may contain some differing emphases. In Part Two, the online faculty portfolio review process used by the Organization Management and Development program at Fielding Graduate University is presented as a sample of how portfolio review for online faculty may be conducted.

## PROGRAM EVALUATION

Certainly, course and faculty evaluation are significant components of the evaluation of an online program. There are additional factors that should be considered when completing a comprehensive program review, however, and we will now discuss the most important of them: competency mapping. Johnson, Wilkes, Ormond, and Figueroa (2002) suggest that curriculum and faculty committees charged with such tasks need to ask themselves the following questions to determine whether curricular revision is, in fact, necessary:

- Does the curriculum meet stakeholder needs?
- Does content level build appropriately across the curriculum?
- Is there improper and unnecessary duplication of content?
- Does class content match the described curriculum?
- What other departments utilize a given course?
- What nondiscipline courses are required for the degree, and are they readily available?
- Do discipline and nondiscipline courses support one another?
- What are the implications if a course is deleted?

The responses to these questions help to set the stage for a competency mapping project. In Chapter One we discussed the means by which competencies are developed, and we provide a brief example of how to map competencies to outcomes to objectives. In a larger competency mapping project, however, the goal is to graphically illustrate how the competencies developed for the program are addressed in every course in the program. The development of competencies is accomplished through a consensus-building process wherein numerous mechanisms are tapped for input. These can include the following:

- Student surveys
- Standardized tests
- Employer surveys
- Required professional competencies for practice
- Alumni surveys
- Student assessments and analysis of final projects required for the program
- Portfolio analyses
- Job placement tracking

Once the competencies are agreed on and established, then a process to evaluate how well they are being accomplished is put in place. First, as mentioned earlier, the competencies are mapped to each course in which they appear. Then feedback mechanisms that help to measure achievement of the students' competencies must be put in place. Often this mechanism is a final integrative project, thesis, or capstone course that involves the demonstrated application of the competencies. The results can then be analyzed to determine areas of the curriculum that are working well, need improvement, or might be missing. The process, then, is as follows:

- Establish competencies that address desired goals of the program and are responsive to the marketplace in which students will eventually be hired.
- Develop a set of competency-curriculum maps that link each competency to a course or course unit.
- Develop feedback mechanisms designed to measure the achievement of outcomes.
- Analyze the results of the feedback mechanisms to identify areas of the curriculum in need of attention.
- Modify the curriculum in the areas of need.
- Begin the cycle again.

The use of this process helps ensure that regular program reviews occur, keeps the focus on outcomes and competency development, and keeps the process learner focused. It is a comprehensive means by which courses and programs can be evaluated on an ongoing basis.

## COMPETENCY ASSESSMENT AS COURSE AND PROGRAM EVALUATION

The American Psychological Association (APA, 2007) presents recommendations for best practices in assessment that link to competency assessment and can form the foundation for an ongoing evaluation program, such as the one we have just presented. Their recommendations also form a good summary of all we have been discussing regarding course and program evaluation. We now review and add comments about each of their ten recommendations.

### Encourage Department Ownership to Drive the Process

To design effective assessment programs that span all course offerings and that can become a foundation of program evaluation, all faculty need to be engaged in the process. The APA notes that "assessment planning should grow out of the fundamental questions the faculty have about how their contributions shape program success" (para. 1). The more ownership faculty feel for the process, the more likely they are to participate in the development of a consistent approach across courses and to voluntarily participate in peer review and portfolio review programs. Administrators, then, should work in collaboration with the faculty to determine how best to assess and evaluate in a comprehensive way.

### Define Your Objectives in the Context of Your Institutional Mission

As Dunn, Morgan, O'Reilly, and Parry (2004) note, the development of competencies, outcomes, objectives, and assessments begins with the organizational mission and asks the questions, "What do we want our graduates to be when they leave us? What do we want them to represent?" Just as with organizational strategic planning, in which the mission drives organizational objectives, the mission of the institution should drive the evaluation of competencies and outcomes. Additionally, many institutions are engaging in a strategic planning process for online programs. This is a wise undertaking in that the development of competencies, outcomes, and objectives will be part and parcel of this process and will help to standardize and implement them across all courses offered in the online program. This not only will assist students in knowing what to expect but also will create a solid foundation for program review by external bodies, such as accrediting agencies.

### Focus on Collaboration and Teamwork

The APA notes, "Collaboration within the department, across departments, and with higher administration will facilitate the best outcomes from assessment planning" (para. 3). In this way, assessment and evaluation become institution-wide activities that drive practice, create consistency across courses and programs, and help to create alignment that promotes student satisfaction with the learning process. Once again, alignment and consistency are the keys and should be the driving force behind good assessment and evaluation.

### Clarify the Purpose of Assessment

We have already spent considerable time earlier in the book discussing this very important concept—however, the APA states that students should experience positive benefit from the assessment activities in which they are engaged. This clearly shifts the focus from a faculty-focused assessment to a learner-centered one. The learners should always be the center of attention in conducting assessment or evaluation. It is their learning process that is paramount.

### Identify Clear, Measurable, and Developmental Student Learning

Developing assessment criteria at a departmental or institutional level helps to create coherence with desired program competencies and the institutional mission. As much as possible, assessment criteria should be developed more broadly than at the course level to reduce subjectivity and facilitate program evaluation. As we have noted, instructors also need to incorporate into their courses ways to measure developmental progress toward program competencies and institutional mission.

### Use Multiple Measures and Sources Consistent with Resources

Program evaluation is research, and, as most researchers know, employing multiple measures ensures more valid results. Consequently, a good evaluation program should include ways by which competencies and outcomes can be measured that go beyond student performance. Good course evaluations should be designed that are not popularity assessments but actually look at how the course and instructor contributed to student learning. Peer reviews and portfolio reviews should be employed to determine the impact of good teaching practice as well as to serve as professional development. Finally, the use of outside evaluators, including program alumni and employers who are hiring graduates, can assist in reducing subjectivity.

### Implement Continuous Assessment with Clear, Manageable Timelines

Regular review of both student and program outcomes can promote continuous quality improvement, thus contributing to student satisfaction with the learning process and increased student retention and completion. Reviews should be scheduled and the schedule adhered to in order not to lose sight of continuous quality improvement.

### Help Students Succeed on Assessment Tasks

As Walvoord and Anderson (1998) note, clear assignment and grading criteria help students to complete assignments successfully. The ability to receive feedback throughout the course also contributes to positive performance on final assessments. Implementing these practices across courses helps to increase student success. Additionally, provision of student support services helps students to achieve goals and objectives. One aspect of program review is a determination of what resources are supporting student success and what might be missing but necessary. For example, if program evaluation reveals a need for student writing assistance, how will that be provided? The response to that question then becomes part of the ongoing review process.

### Interpret and Use Assessment Results Appropriately

The APA cautions, "Assessment should be a stimulus for growth, renewal, and improvement, not an action that generates data to ensure positive outcomes" (para. 9). Although it is wonderful to be able to use assessment and evaluation activities as ways to pat ourselves on the back for a job well done, it is also critical to explore the areas of need that emerge. As such, the results of assessment and evaluation activities should be used as benchmarks for success, improvement, or both.

### Evaluate Your Assessment Practices

Again, because evaluation of assessment practice is a form of action research, every effort should be made to ensure reliability, validity, and usefulness.

Through our actions of using assessment and evaluation for continuous quality improvement and looking closely at developing consistent practices across departments and the college or university as a whole, poor assessment practice should become obvious, promoting opportunities for professional development in this area.

## APPLYING WHAT WE HAVE LEARNED

This book has thus far provided a look at the foundations of good assessment and evaluation while keeping a learner focus. It is clear that although many principles of traditional face-to-face assessment and evaluation also apply online, the different nature of online instruction requires that different approaches be used in assessment and evaluation. As we have noted many times over, simply moving techniques that might work well in the face-to-face classroom to the online environment is likely doomed to failure and creates problems and concerns that then must be addressed, such as the increase in potential problems with security and decreased instructor confidence in the integrity of assessment. Likewise, instructor performance online cannot be measured by traditional means, because what is required of instructors changes when they enter the online classroom. Finally, a learner-centered approach to instruction, which is the preferred means by which online instruction is conceived, begs for a learner-centered approach to assessment and evaluation. The goal of constructivist, adult-oriented learning situations is coconstructed knowledge and meaning. Therefore, the more we involve our learners in the development of assessment and evaluation activities, the more empowered they become as learners, scholars, and practitioners, and the more satisfied they will be with their learning experience.

The following comments, offered by a faculty member at Delgado Community College—who was a student in our Teaching in the Virtual Classroom (TVC) program— beautifully sum up thoughts about assessment and competency attainment:

> In my last post I talked about HOW we learned—our constructivist online learning community—in this course.
>
> Upon further reflection, I thought I should comment on WHAT I learned, because I learned some important things that have transformed my thinking and redirected my educational agenda.

As a teacher providing individual instruction to graduate voice and conducting students, and undergraduate voice students, or as a conductor directing the Symphony Chorus of New Orleans or the Delgado College Choir, I have always relied on my ability to improvise teaching strategies in response to individual or group dynamics. This program has not changed my approach to this part of my life very much. This part of my teaching has always been outcomes-based and learning-centered: There's a concert coming up, and they've got to learn the music and the skills needed to perform it in public. As a conductor, or when accompanying my students on the piano, I am not just presenting the work of others—my artistic product and integrity are on the line—out there for all to judge, too.

However, in face-to-face and online teaching, my attitude and strategies have changed a great deal. Some of this is related to learning-centeredness in general, but much of it is specific learning in response to the TVC program.

The first paradigm shift I have experienced is that the purpose of assessment is improvement of learning. In the past, I have simply followed the received knowledge that the purpose of evaluation is accountability. It should come as no surprise that the questions we ask and the vocabulary we use affect not only the answers we get but how we get to them. This has led me to subject every aspect of my teaching to the question, "How does this improve learning?"

The second is that critical reflection is assessment. This has opened the door to including more writing in all my classes and to facilitating discussion in my online classes. It provides a way around the poor preparation for writing that many of my students display. It also allows me to distinguish between high-stakes writing (paper) and low-stakes writing (discussion).

Specifically dealing with online instruction, social presence cannot happen unless the course design and instructor's facilitation make it happen. Actually this is pretty much true of everything related to course design in the online environment. It is unreasonable to expect that students will intuit what has not been made clear and explicit in the absence of facial expression and other social clues or modeling. This situation also prevents the instructor from intervening and

> assisting the lost student. Best put it all up front and clarify expectations and offer opportunities for communication.
>
> —*Steven*

Steven's reflections indicate to us that the competencies we set forth for the program were achieved. Steven has begun to question all of his teaching practice to ensure learner-centeredness and has realized the important function that assessment plays in both online and face-to-face teaching. Assessment bridges the gap between what was taught and what was learned, and in the online classroom, *how* it was taught is also critical to that process.

With these thoughts in mind, the following are the key principles we have presented in this chapter:

- Course and program evaluation should be based on the mission of the institution, program competencies, and course outcomes.
- Course, faculty, and program evaluation should be an ongoing activity that provides a solid foundation for continuous quality improvement.
- Collaboration between faculty and administrators is necessary to ensure a comprehensive, institution-wide program of course and program evaluation.
- Multiple measures should be used to effectively evaluate online efforts at the course and program levels.
- Course, faculty, and program evaluation must be learner-focused—it is the learning process that is most important and of the most value.
- A comprehensive program of course, faculty, and program evaluation ensures rigor and quality and that best practices will be employed in every aspect of course and program delivery.

We now move to the second part of this book, the Assessment and Evaluation Toolkit, which provides activities, tips, and examples of assessment and evaluation activities based on the learner-focused theoretical frame we have presented. We invite readers to use them in the development of their own assessment and evaluation program, and we welcome feedback on their application and use.

PART TWO

# The Assessment and Evaluation Toolkit

## INTRODUCTION TO THE ASSESSMENT AND EVALUATION TOOLKIT

The Assessment and Evaluation Toolkit is a review of the assessment and evaluation techniques we have been discussing to this point, with the addition of tips and tricks for their implementation in online courses and programs. The toolkit is designed as a stand-alone resource for readers to use as they see fit. Many of the assessment techniques contain worksheets or guiding questions, which may be used as is or adapted to fit the needs of the course. We also include examples of assessment activities developed by our participants in the Teaching in the Virtual Classroom program at Fielding Graduate University, all of whom are online instructors themselves or aspiring to teach online. These activities illustrate some of the forms of assessment that we have been discussing in the book. Some of the tools we present are original works of our own design that we have been using successfully in our own online courses. Others are adaptations from the work of our colleagues; we have acknowledged them as appropriate. We are grateful for their contributions and for the good work they are doing in the area of assessment.

The toolkit contains presentations of the following assessment techniques:

- Rubric design and development, including sample rubrics
- The use of student feedback in assessment
- A rubric for faculty and instructional designers looking at the degree of learner-centeredness and interactivity a course may have
- The use of authentic assessments
- The use of performance assessments
- Effective test and quiz development
- Portfolio assessments
- Self-assessment
- Peer assessment
- Collaborative assessment
- Reflective assessment
- The use of wikis and blogs in assessment
- Effective course evaluation
- Effective faculty evaluation

Some resources are included in the discussions in the toolkit. Following the toolkit, however, is a section of Additional Resources in the form of websites, software, and articles and books that may be useful to the instructor who is developing an assessment scheme for an online course or for an administrator who is developing course and program evaluation materials.

## RUBRICS AND RUBRIC DEVELOPMENT

Rubrics have become a useful tool in the assessment of student work online. They provide clarity in expectations for student performance and assist in turning subjective assessments of assignments, such as responses to discussion questions, into more objective measures of student work. Consequently, developing skill in the design of rubrics is important. The following material is provided in order to simplify and demystify the process of rubric development.

### Designing Rubrics

Stevens and Levi (2004) delineate four stages involved in rubric development for any assignment:

1. *Reflecting.* Take some time to think about the expectations for the assignment. What are the expectations and how will they be communicated to learners?
2. *Listing.* Once the expectations have been determined, begin to develop learning objectives. What are the details and learning objectives for this assignment?
3. *Grouping and Labeling.* Next, group similar expectations and skills, then label them according to performance levels. What are the categories of expectations and how are performance levels determined? What constitutes basic performance, for example? What constitutes proficiency? What would exceptional performance look like?
4. *Application.* Apply the skills and labels from Step 3 to the grid format of the final rubric.

The sections that follow provide more detail to assist with the rubric development process.

## Determining Gradable Activities

As the course is being developed, consider the activities that will be assessed and graded. The following are elements to consider:

- Activities should directly relate to course learning objectives.
- All course activities should relate to one another.
- Activities should be based on previous experience with like assignments.
- Activities should relate to the skill set of students entering the course or should help develop new skills.

Thinking about the activities in this way should help to delineate learning objectives for the activities being developed as well as provide a means to link them to course outcomes.

## Determining Performance Levels for Activities

The following questions assist in determining the desired performance levels on activities:

- What evidence can students provide that would show they have accomplished what you want them to? In other words, what does proficiency look like?
- What are the highest expectations for student performance? In other words, what would exceptional (generally termed *distinguished*) performance look like?
- What is the worst performance you can imagine beyond not doing the assignment at all?

## Using Rubrics in Assessment

The following is an example of how a rubric for online discussion might be introduced and used in an online course:

> Attached is a rubric for participation in online discussions. The way to use this rubric is to look at the "gradable" items listed down the left-hand side of the grid. Across the top are the performance levels, which roughly (and I do mean roughly!) equate to grades.
>
> To earn an A, for example, you would not need to fill in all of the boxes down the right-hand column—your performance in discussions

might be extremely strong with a combination of items from the *two* columns on the right (Proficient and Distinguished) and maybe even one item that you feel shows basic performance. The idea is to look at the total picture of your discussion performance.

So, at mid-term and again at the end of the term, what I want you to do is to send me an e-mail (I'll nudge you at mid-term) telling me where you think you fall on the rubric. For example, you might say that for including and applying course concepts and theories, you feel that you fall into the proficient category, while you feel you are distinguished in applying real-world examples and applications of the theories. You'll go through each category and tell me where you think you fall on the grid. I don't generally give mid-term grades, so what I'll be doing is responding to your e-mail with my own assessment based on your self-assessment. I hope that's not too confusing! If there's a discrepancy in our perceptions, we'll discuss it. If we agree, then great!

At the end of the term, I'm going to ask you to do this again. But, this time, I'm going to ask you to tell me what grade you think you've earned as well. Questions about this? Please ask!

### Reconciling Differences

Rubrics define how grades will be determined, thus reducing conflicting opinions and grade appeals. If differences occur, however, students should be encouraged to use the rubric to illustrate how they see their performance differently from the way in which the instructor sees it. This opens discussion between the instructor and student that can lead to performance improvement and clarification of expectations.

### Sample Grading Rubrics for Course Activities

The following are two sample rubrics. One shows a blank grid that can be used for any type of assignment. The second is a sample rubric for a class presentation.

In the examples of types of lessons and related assessments that follow in this section of the book, we include grading rubrics that accompany the lessons to provide further examples of ways in which to develop and apply rubrics.

## DESCRIPTION OF ACTIVITY/ASSIGNMENT:

| Criteria (__ Total Points or Percentage of Total) | 0 Nonperformance | 1 Basic | 2 Proficient | 3 Distinguished |
|---|---|---|---|---|
| | | | | |

### Grading Scale:

[The points-to-grade scale should be included here.]

## DESCRIPTION OF ACTIVITY/ASSIGNMENT:

Presentation to class based on research of chosen topic.

| Criteria (__ Total Points or Percentage of Total) | 0 Nonperformance | 1 Basic | 2 Proficient | 3 Distinguished |
|---|---|---|---|---|
| Knowledge/ Understanding 50% or 50 points | | | | |
| Thinking/Inquiry 30% or 30 points | | | | |
| Communication of Ideas 20% or 20 points | | | | |

### Grading Scale:

[The points-to-grade scale should be included here.]

## USING STUDENT FEEDBACK FOR ASSESSMENT

The following are tips for promoting and using student feedback as part of assessment activities:

- Develop course guidelines that include an expectation of students' feedback to one another.
- Promote a sense of collaboration rather than competition through the use of feedback.
- Encourage posting of feedback on the discussion board rather than through e-mail, as this allows instructors to see material not otherwise available.
- Explain the importance of giving good feedback: it deepens the level of discussion and learning.

### Developing Good Feedback Techniques

Students need orientation on how to give and receive feedback. The following are points that should be stressed in teaching students about how to give good feedback.

Feedback should:

- Respond to the question in a way that clearly supports a position
- Begin a new topic
- Add to the discussion by critically reflecting on what is being discussed
- Move the discussion in a new direction
- Ask a question to stimulate further thinking on the part of the person to whom the feedback is addressed

### Feedback Guidelines for Students

- Don't just make feedback up as you go along. Plan ahead.
- Before you start to type, first think about what you want to say. Get your ideas straight in your head and figure out how they all fit together.

- Make some notes before typing a message online. This helps you figure out what you need to say.
- Use short paragraphs. This forces you to express yourself with a minimum of words.
- When you write something, make sure that people will understand you. After you type a message—and before you send it—try reading it out loud. Sometimes sentences that seem to be okay when you're typing don't really work when you read them back.
- Some people quote a huge message, then place a brief comment at the end, such as "I agree with this!" or "Me, too!" This can be annoying to the person who has to scroll all the way through the message, looking for the part that you wrote. It makes more sense for you to quote only a few important sentences that summarize the message adequately, and place your comment after that.
- Simply saying that you agree with something doesn't add much to the conversation. Why not tell people *why* you agree? You can state some of the reasons why you feel the way you do. This way, you will look like a thoughtful person who thinks carefully about things and considers all the facts.
- You should always read what you have written before you send your message. Not only will this help you spot errors in spelling, phrasing, and grammar but also you may notice that you don't sound as friendly as you would like. Make sure your message is worded professionally and not harshly to avoid insulting those who will read it and inadvertently "flaming" other members of the group. (Palloff & Pratt, 2003, pp. 171–172)

## HOW INTERACTIVE IS IT?

The following rubric is an adaptation of Roblyer and Wiencke's (2003) rubric for assessing interaction in online courses. We contend that courses can be highly interactive without the use of such technologies as audio and video conferencing; consequently we have eliminated that category of evaluation. This rubric shows ways in which interactivity can be evaluated. The points can be totaled and used as part of a faculty self-assessment or administrative assessment of the effectiveness of the course and faculty performance.

| Scale (points) | Development of Social Presence | Instructional Design for Interaction | Evidence of Learner Engagement | Evidence of Instructor Engagement |
|---|---|---|---|---|
| Low (1) | No attempts made—no intros, bios, or use of collaboration. No presence of a café area in the course. | Students communicate only with instructor via e-mail. Content presented in "lecture" format through text and graphics. No use of discussion board and no required interaction between learners. | Learners respond to instructor as required but do not respond to one another. | Instructor responds to learner assignments but does not promote additional discussion. |
| Minimum (2) | Intros and bios are required. | Minimal use of discussion board, but discussion is required—students are asked to choose discussion questions to respond to, or discussion assignments occur at intervals rather than weekly. | Learners respond to discussion questions and, as required, to other learners. There is little evidence of voluntary discussion outside of assignments. | Instructor posts an expectation of timely feedback to learners, responds to learner assignments, and is present on the discussion board. Instructor may respond to every post, limiting student-to-student engagement. |
| Average (3) | Intros and bios are required. An ice-breaker activity is included at the start of a course. | Discussion is a regular part of the course. Students are required to respond to discussion questions and to at least one or two peers weekly. Discussion may or may not be assessed. | Learners respond to discussion questions and provide minimum required feedback to peers that demonstrates application of course concepts. Some voluntary discussion beyond assignments is present, with indicators that a learning community has formed. | Instructor posts an expectation of timely feedback to learners, responds to learner assignments, and demonstrates some ability to promote learner-to-learner discussion through strategic response that summarizes or links student posts to extend discussion. Instructor shows some ability to develop a learning community. |

| | | | | |
|---|---|---|---|---|
| Above Average (4) | Intros and bios are required. Instructor responds to intros and bios as a model for students. An ice-breaker activity is included at the start of a course, and a café area is included in the course. | Discussion is a regular part of the course. Students are required to respond to discussion questions and at least two of their peers weekly. Dyad or small group assignments are included in the course design. Discussion is part of the assessment scheme for the course. | Learners respond to discussion questions and to their peers and initiate discussion that goes beyond the assignments. Learner postings are substantive, show application of course concepts, and indicate engagement with course material and one another. There are indicators that a learning community has formed. | Instructor posts clear expectations of response to learner e-mails and assignments within a designated timeframe, demonstrates good ability to promote learner-to-learner discussion through strategic response to discussions, and offers additional materials for consideration. Instructor shows ability to develop and maintain a learning community. |
| High (5) | Intros and bios are required. Instructor responds to intros and bios as a model for students and may use audio or video as part of the instructor intro. An ice-breaker activity is included at the start of a course. A café area is included in the course and students are encouraged to engage with one another and the instructor in the café through informal discussion. | Discussion is a regular part of the course and is assessed. Students are required to respond to discussion questions and at least two of their peers weekly. Dyad or small group assignments are included in the course design. The use of synchronous discussion media may be included. | Learners respond to discussion questions and to their peers and initiate discussion that goes beyond the assignments. Learner postings are substantive, show application and evaluation of course concepts, and indicate engagement with course material and one another. Learners engage in informal communications through the café area of the course and show both strong connections to one another and the presence of a learning community. | Instructor posts clear expectations of response to learner e-mails and assignments, responds to learner e-mails within twenty-four to forty-eight hours and to assignments within seven days, demonstrates good ability to promote learner-to-learner discussion through strategic response to discussions, and offers additional materials for consideration. Instructor shows good ability to develop and maintain a learning community. |

Points to determine level of interactivity: Low – 1 to 8; Average – 9 to 15; High – 16 to 20.

## AUTHENTIC ASSESSMENTS

The following are features of authentic assessments:

- Generally take the form of application activities, such as simulations, role playing, or use of case studies
- Effectively demonstrate not only acquisition of knowledge but ability to apply that knowledge in professional or other settings
- Are effectively assessed through the use of rubrics

The following are guidelines in the use of authentic assessments:

- Learner performance is to be evaluated under the same conditions and using the same materials as a real-world performance would present.
- Students are equal partners in the learning and assessment processes; that is, the activity is collaborative and assessed collaboratively.
- Students perceive the value of the assessment, as it demands real-world performance of learning.
- Students are motivated to participate, as the activity closely aligns with learning objectives and outcomes.

The following is an example of an authentic assessment created by Jeffrey Strauser, who teaches Health Science at Jamestown Community College:

### CHAPTER 23 – ENVIRONMENTAL HEALTH. ENERGY POLICY.

The Year is 2016. The United States is in a true energy crisis. There are electrical brownouts and blackouts everywhere (meaning some areas have limited or no electricity available). Gasoline is now being rationed. Because of this, Congress has authorized an Emergency Energy Commission with extraordinary powers to alleviate this energy crisis. This committee will report directly to the President of the United States. As fate would have it, the members of this class are the commission members. Congress stipulated the commission members will be divided into two task forces. Task Force A will be tasked with coming up with a minimum of five methods to obtain more energy for Americans to use. Task Force B will be tasked with developing a minimum of five methods for Americans to conserve energy. It is hoped that, by working both sides of the energy equation, we can alleviate our energy crisis.

Class members can choose which task force they would like to be in, but we do need seven members in each group. Each task force will pick a leader to help coordinate their group. This being a summer class, we have only ten days to complete our task. Use Chapter 23, Environmental Health as your first reference to get you started. To complete this assignment, you will need to use additional reputable sources of information.

Task Force A must come up with a minimum of five ways to increase the energy supplies of the United States. Every member needs to contribute. Justify each method you come up with.

Task Force B must develop a minimum of five methods for Americans to conserve energy. Every member needs to contribute. Justify each method you develop.

After each task force posts its lists with the justifications, we need Task Force A to critique Task Force B's list and justifications and vice versa.

Each discussion post is graded according to the following rubric:

| Points | Interpretation | Grading Criteria |
|---|---|---|
| 9–10 | Excellent (A) | The comment is accurate, original, relevant, and well written, and it teaches. |
| 8–9 | Above Average (B) | The comment lacks at least one of the above qualities, but is above average in quality. |
| 7–8 | Average (C) | The comment lacks two or three of the required qualities. Comments based on personal opinion or personal experience often fall within this category. |
| 6–7 | Minimal (D) | The comment presents little or no new information; however, it may provide social presence and contribute to a collegial atmosphere. |
| Less than 6 | Unacceptable (F) | The comment adds no value to the discussion. |

The second example of an authentic assessment is presented by Kirk Pinnock, from Excelsior Community College in Kingston, Jamaica. Kirk notes that he has used case studies in his face-to-face classes for many years. He finds cases on the Internet and in various textbooks and adapts them for class use. This case was further adapted for online delivery.

## *TOPIC:* INTRODUCTION TO NETWORKS

*Instructor:* Kirk Pinnock, Excelsior Community College

*Description:* The purpose of this lesson is to provide students with a framework to develop their knowledge and understanding of simple computer networks.

### Learning objectives

At the end of the lesson the students should be able to

- Understand and describe the differences between stand-alone and networked computers
- Describe the advantages and disadvantages of different network topologies
- Demonstrate understanding of the purpose of a range of hardware and software used to create and maintain network environments

### Previous knowledge

Students taking this course should already

- Know the basic components of a stand-alone computer system
- Know how to browse the Internet and search for information online
- Know how to use presentation software

### Activities

**Introduction** *Kadian Arthurs has been in business as a gardening supplies retailer for six years. She has just opened her own nursery adjacent to her store and also a second store across town. She is pleased that her business is doing so well. Two years ago, she bought her first computer and printer and has used them successfully to keep sales records in a* *spreadsheet and produce flyers and leaflets using a desktop publishing package.*

*She has seen how useful computers can be and wants to buy several more. She thinks that she will need three more computers at her main shop and two at the new store.*

*Kadian has read about computer networks in a computer magazine and thinks that they sound like a good idea, but she has no idea where to start.*

**Instructions**

1. Before starting the case scenario discussion, make a post to the threaded discussion forum, defining the term *network* and identifying the essential components of a network, citing a real-world example that illustrates what a network is. In addition to the assigned reading, share one resource that you found relevant to the topic being discussed. Read the posts of your classmates and comment on at least two of their posts.
2. *Kadian has asked you to find out about the differences between standalone and networked computers. She is keen to network the four computers at her main shop, but wants to make sure she is not wasting her money.*

   Write a business memo to Kadian detailing the advantages and disadvantages of the two different approaches (networking and stand-alone) and making the case for a small network. Post your final memo to the forum. Read and comment on the posts of your fellow learners as the week progresses.
3. *Kadian has heard that there are two different ways that her network could be set up, either as a* peer-to-peer *or as a* client-server *network.*

   In groups of three, produce a short presentation (using your presentation software) to describe the differences between peer-to-peer and client-server networks. What hardware and software will Kadian need?

   Post your final presentation to the forum. The preparation forum should be used to brainstorm about information to present in the final presentation.

A list of the persons in each group will be posted mid-afternoon on the second day of the week.

4. *Kadian is ready to proceed.*

   You now need to research three different network topologies (bus, ring, and star) and extend the presentation your group prepared in Task 3 to describe the benefits and drawbacks of each one. Your presentation should end with a recommendation to Kadian on which network topology she should use in her store and an explanation why this is the best one. Review the presentations of the other groups and comment on the suitability of the proposed solutions.

## Assessment

**Participation** Participation will account for 20 percent of the final grade for this lesson. Each student is automatically allotted 2 percent on starting the lesson.

| Criteria | Unacceptable 0 Points | Acceptable 1 Point | Good 2 Points | Excellent 3 Points |
|---|---|---|---|---|
| **Frequency** | Participates not at all. | Participates one or two times on the same day. | Participates three or four times but postings not distributed throughout week. | Participates four or five times throughout the week. |
| **Initial Assignment Posting** | Posts no assignment. | Posts an adequate assignment with superficial thought and preparation; doesn't address all aspects of the task. | Posts a well-developed assignment that addresses all aspects of the task; lacks full development of concepts. | Posts a well-developed assignment that fully addresses and develops all aspects of the task. |
| **Follow-Up Postings** | Posts no follow-up responses to others. | Posts a shallow contribution to the discussion (for example, simply agrees or disagrees); does not enrich discussion. | Elaborates on an existing posting with further comment or observation. | Demonstrates analysis of others' posts; extends meaningful discussion by building on previous posts. |

| Criteria | Unacceptable<br>0 Points | Acceptable<br>1 Point | Good<br>2 Points | Excellent<br>3 Points |
|---|---|---|---|---|
| **Content Contribution** | Posts information that is off topic, incorrect, or irrelevant to the discussion. | Repeats but does not add substantive information to the discussion. | Posts information that is factually correct; lacks full development of concept or thought. | Posts a factually correct, reflective, and substantive contribution; advances discussion. |
| **References and Support** | Includes no references or supporting experience. | Uses personal experience, but no references to readings or research. | Incorporates some references from literature and personal experience. | Uses references to literature, readings, or personal experience to support comments. |
| **Clarity and Mechanics** | Posts long, unorganized, or rude content that may contain multiple errors or may be inappropriate. | Communicates in a friendly, courteous, and helpful manner, with some errors in clarity or mechanics. | Contributes valuable information to the discussion, with minor clarity or mechanics errors. | Contributes to discussion with clear, concise comments formatted in an easy-to-read style free of grammatical or spelling errors. |

## Presentation – 20 Percent

The final presentation (Task 4) will account for 40 percent of the final grade (Score × 2).

| Beginning<br>1 Point | Developing<br>2 Points | Accomplished<br>3 Points | Exemplary<br>4 Points | Score |
|---|---|---|---|---|
| Understanding of Key Issues | Superficial or obvious issues are correctly identified but more complex issues are ignored. | Superficial as well as some deeper issues are identified and correctly explained in the presentation. | All major issues (both superficial and complex) are identified and correctly explained in the presentation. | Superficial and complex issues are identified, and subtle nuances of the issues are explained insightfully. |

(*Continued*)

| | Beginning 1 Point | Developing 2 Points | Accomplished 3 Points | Exemplary 4 Points | Score |
|---|---|---|---|---|---|
| Creativity of Recommendations | The solution either is not relevant to the problem or is only a restatement of some preexisting solution. | The recommendation is a simple synthesis of at least two commonly known recommendations. | The recommendation synthesizes multiple existing proposals in a manner not previously proposed. | The recommendation appears to generate new ideas in conjunction with synthesis of common recommendations of others. | |
| Effectiveness of Argument | The case made for the group's proposal overlooks major points or key information, or lacks coherence. The plan does not seem likely to work based on the argument presented. | The proposal seems to speak to all the major points and may be workable but some elements of the plan may lack clarity or needed documentation supporting the proposal. | The proposal includes explanations and documentation that are generally relevant to all the major elements of the problem being investigated, and appears to be workable. | The proposal is well organized, considers all major points and nuances, and includes ample documentation to justify the positions taken, and appears likely to result in a workable solution for many (if not all) of the constituent groups. | |
| Aesthetic Quality of Presentation | Presentation is unattractive or presentation tools (such as Microsoft PowerPoint) are not used consistently throughout the presentation, or the presentation does not work correctly. | Presentation tools are used to create and deliver a working presentation in which most of the major points are explained and most include effective use of graphic layout and design. | Presentation tools are used to create and deliver a working presentation in which all of the major points are explained using elements that communicate effectively and follow basic principles of design. | Attractive and original elements enhance a well organized and fully working presentation. Major points are made more clear through effective use of graphics and design principles. | |
| Teamwork | Team members do not work together to make the presentation. | Team members work together to make the presentation. | Team members work as a group to make the presentation. | Team members work as a cohesive unit to make the presentation. | |

### Business Memo

This task contributes 20 percent of the final grade.

| Trait | 1 Point | 3 Points | 5 Points |
|---|---|---|---|
| Content | Purpose unclear, incomplete, inaccurate<br>Facts not supported<br>Audience and information do not match at all | Purpose unclear<br>Not all facts supported<br>Audience and information don't match as well | Purpose clear, complete, accurate<br>Facts supported<br>Audience and information match |
| Organization | Reader likely to be confused<br>No main points<br>Key information difficult to locate | Straightforward manner<br>Main points inferred or don't stand out<br>Key information can be located with a little work | Information is pertinent<br>Main points stand out<br>Key information easy to spot |
| Style and Terminology | Language unclear<br>Technical terms clutter text or are unnecessary | Language occasionally unclear<br>Technical terms sometimes used when not needed | Language clear<br>Technical terms and vocabulary used only when necessary |
| Format, Layout, and Conventions | Layout cluttered<br>Key ideas not emphasized<br>Graphics needed, not used<br>Not mailable; spelling errors | Appropriate layout<br>Key ideas emphasized inefficiently<br>Graphics minimal<br>Mailable with reservation; no spelling errors | Layout attractive and balanced<br>Key ideas stand out (bold, italics, numbered list)<br>Uses graphics when needed<br>Free from error (mailable document) |

## PERFORMANCE ASSESSMENTS

The following are criteria for the use of performance assessments:

- Students will create a product or demonstrate a skill that is connected to the learning process.
- The performance will occur in a complex environment.

- The performance demonstrates higher-order thinking and problem-solving skills.
- The activity stimulates a range of responses.
- The activity is challenging and requires student time and effort.

The following example of a performance assessment was created by Juanita Robinson, a community college instructor in computer applications.

## WORD PROJECT: MODIFYING AN ANNOUNCEMENT

*Purpose:* To demonstrate the ability to modify an announcement by formatting, importing, and scaling a graphic from clip art; using the spell checker; saving; and printing.

*Problem:* You are the Assistant Director of Alumni Relations for Sunny Valley College. The Alumni Relations Director has asked you to use your word processing skills to modify an existing document to promote an upcoming tour of the Far East by members of the Alumni Association.

*Instructions:* Modify the announcement by following these instructions:

1. Open the file Word Project from a location provided by your instructor.
2. Make sure the first title is left-aligned, bold and italicize it, and change its font to Arial and its font size to 28.
3. Right-align the second title line, bold it, change its font to Arial, and change the font size to 18.
4. From the travel category in clip art, insert the air travel clip art beneath the second title line. Select and center the picture.
5. Change the font size of the first three paragraphs under the graphic to 14 points. They begin with the words "Leaving international," "The tour," and "Deadline for your deposit."
6. Center the words "Call 555-8900 for more information." Change the font to Arial and bold.

7. Bold, underline, and center the registration form title, "Far Eastern Tour Reservation Form."
8. Bold and underline the words "SVC Alumni Association" that appear in the registration form.
9. Make the following changes:
   a. In the first paragraph under the graphic, change the departure date from June 24, 2004 to June 23, 2009.
   b. In the first paragraph under the graphic, change Singapore to Hong Kong.
   c. Change the deposit from $250 to $300. This amount appears twice in the document: in the third paragraph under the graphic and in the registration form.
   d. In the fourth paragraph under the graphic, change the deadline date from June 1 to June 3.
10. Check the spelling of the announcement.
11. At the bottom of the document, beneath the address, type your name and the date, separated by commas.
12. Save the announcement with the file name Lab Test #1.
13. Print the announcement.

The following is the announcement to modify using Word:

**Far Eastern Tour**

Sunny Valley College Alumni Association

Leaving International Airport on Saturday, June 24, 2004, the Sunny Valley College Alumni Association will sponsor a tour of the Far East visiting Japan, Singapore, and Australian.

The tour is limited to 74 alumni and their guests.

Your deposit of $250 per person guarantees your ticket to the adventure of a lifetime. The final cost will be $1,100 per person and includes two meals a day plus hotel accommodations.

Deadline for reservations is June 1

Call 555-8900 for more information.

**Far Eastern Tour Reservation Form**

Name (please print)

______________________________________________

Guest Name (one guest per alumnus)

______________________________

Address

______________________________________________

City ______________________ State ________ Zip ________

Telephone ________________________

Make checks payable to: SVC Alumni Association

Mail this coupon and your $250/per person check to:

SVC Alumni Office

1234 Redline Lane

Green Acres, IN 46302

---

The following is a more complex performance assessment conducted collaboratively and resulting in the production of a group "fishbone" diagram.

## FISHBONE ASSIGNMENT AND ACTIVITY

*Instructor:* Martha Davidson

*Purpose of Lesson:* To explore Total Quality Management (TQM) and the cause-and-effect analysis (fishbone) and enable learners to evaluate problems associated with applying Total Quality Management in academics.

The original philosophy and principles of TQM were developed by Edward Deming. He approached the TQM concept from a business perspective. His purpose was to analyze problems associated with products and services in manufacturing.

Today, quality has become an inherent part of business operations. In production and manufacturing environments, there are laws and statistical process controls to measure and ensure compliance of TQM standards, e.g., ISO 9000 and ISO 14000. However, the educational environment has been slow to fully integrate TQM principles in a similar manner.

An article titled "Applying Total Quality Management in Academics" supported my interest in developing the concept of TQM into a lesson plan. The article states, "The concept of TQM is applicable to academics." Many educators believe that Deming's concept of TQM provides guiding principles for needed educational reform. In his article, "The Quality Revolution in Education," John Jay Bonstingl outlines the TQM principles he believes are most salient to education reform. He calls them the "Four Pillars of Total Quality Management" (Mehrotra, n.d.).

In this lesson, we will explore why TQM has not been fully integrated into academics.

## Resource

"Applying Total Quality Management in Academics" retrieved from website iSixSigma, http://www.isixsigma.com/library/content/c020626a.asp

**Learning Objectives and Outcomes:**

1. Learner will demonstrate an understanding of the theories of TQM and cause-and-effect analyses (fishbone) and apply the techniques to analyze problems associated with applying TQM in academics.
2. Learner will demonstrate the ability to brainstorm through discussion, and use the resources, examples, and processes provided to identify key categories, problems, and the possible main causes and subcauses.
3. Learner will demonstrate the ability to design a fishbone, by using the Fishbone Diagram Generator at www.freequality.org, to construct a cause-and-effect diagram (fishbone). The diagram will contain:
    a. The stated problem (effect): "Applying TQM in academics"
    b. No less than six main categories (causes) of the problems
    c. No less than two causes branching from the main categories (causes); and at least one subcause branching from the cause.

## Assignment or Activity

Read the complete article, "Applying Total Quality Management in Academics" (http://www.isixsigma.com/library/content/c020626a.asp), brainstorm problems with "applying TQM in academics" (stated problem), and construct a fishbone diagram.

## Materials, Action, Conditions

After reading the preceding and following articles and the background of the fishbone (included in the attachment that follows), brainstorm the causes and subcauses of the stated problem via online discussion and generate a fishbone with the Excel-based fishbone diagram generator at www.freequality.org, accessible under "Tools" and "Fishbone Diagram."

Note: If you receive an error message, continue (do not stop); the diagram will appear. On opening Excel, if you still experience problems, you will need to change your macro security level to low for the fishbone diagram generator to work. Follow steps 1 through 4 as noted in the diagram.

## Goal

The goal is to determine six underlying categories as the bases of the causes and subcauses of problems and to construct a fishbone diagram based on the team's analyses, with no fewer than two causes and one subcause.

## Need

One student to volunteer to act as facilitator, leading the brainstorming discussion and generating a final fishbone based on the team's analyses of problems, using the instructions that follow. Each student is required to use the Fishbone Generator to brainstorm and analyze problems to gain experience using the process.

## Reading Assignment

Implementation of TQM Principles and Processes

A preliminary step in TQM implementation is to assess the organization's current reality. Relevant preconditions have to do with the organization's history, its current needs, precipitating events leading to TQM, and the existing employee quality of working life. If the current reality does not include important preconditions, TQM implementation should be delayed until the organization is in a state in which TQM is likely to succeed.

If an organization has a track record of effective responsiveness to the environment, and if it has been able to successfully change the way it operates when needed, TQM will be easier to implement. If an organization has been historically reactive and has no skill at improving its operating systems, there will be both employee skepticism and a lack of skilled change agents. If this condition prevails, a comprehensive program of management and leadership development may be instituted. A management audit is a good assessment tool to identify current levels of organizational functioning and areas in need of change. An organization should be basically healthy before beginning TQM. If it has significant problems, such as a very unstable funding base, weak administrative systems, lack of managerial skill, or poor employee morale, TQM would not be appropriate.

However, a certain level of stress is probably desirable to initiate TQM. People need to feel a need for a change. Kanter (1983) addresses this phenomenon be describing building blocks that are present in effective organizational change. These forces include departures from tradition, a crisis or galvanizing event, strategic decisions, individual "prime movers," and action vehicles. Departures from tradition are activities, usually at lower levels of the organization, which occur when entrepreneurs move outside the normal ways of operating to solve a problem. A crisis, if it is not too disabling, can also help create a sense of urgency, which can mobilize people to act. In the case of TQM, this may be a funding cut or threat, or demands from consumers or other stakeholders for improved quality of service. After a crisis, a leader may intervene strategically by articulating a new vision of the future to help the organization deal with it. A plan to implement TQM may be such a strategic decision. Such a leader may then become a prime mover, who takes charge in championing the new idea and showing others how it will help them get where they want to go. Finally, action vehicles are needed, as are mechanisms or structures to enable the change to occur and become institutionalized (Hashmi, K. 2000–2006).

## Instruction for Brainstorming and Constructing Fishbone

1. State the problem (effect).
2. Brainstorm the major categories of causes of the problem. If this is difficult, use generic headings; for example:
   - People
   - Current situation (culture)
   - Environment
   - Practices
   - Leadership
   - Development initiatives
3. Write the categories of causes as branches from the main arrow.
4. Brainstorm all the possible causes of the problem. Ask: "Why does this happen?" As each idea is given, the facilitator writes it as a branch from the appropriate category. Causes can be written in several places if they relate to several categories.
5. Again ask "why does this happen?" about each cause. Write sub-causes branching off the causes. Continue to ask "Why?" and generate deeper levels of causes. Layers of branches indicate causal relationships.
6. When the group runs out of ideas, focus attention to places on the diagram where ideas are few.
7. Color branches and twigs using three colors to apply existing link analyses test and measurement data:
   - Green = known not to be a problem
   - Red = definitely a contributing factor but unknown as to degree of causality (may be the only cause or just a contributing cause)
   - Orange = unknown as to whether it contributes to the problem

- Identify the need for additional analysis to determine if the "orange" factors are contributory, and the degree to which the "red" factors are responsible for the problem.
- Conduct additional analyses (discussion) and redraw the diagram, until the causes (red branches) are clearly identified and their relative causality is understood (Skjei, 2005).

8. Save and attach a sample of the team's fishbone to the discussion.
9. Summary—Based on the readings, brainstorming, and problem analysis (fishbone exercise), provide a one- to two-paragraph summary of what you feel would be the primary causes associated with applying TQM in academics at your institution.

## Cause and Effect (Fishbone Diagram)

The fishbone (cause-and-effect) diagram is a problem-solving tool commonly used by quality control teams. Specific causes of problems can be explored through brainstorming. The development of a cause-and-effect diagram requires a team to think through the probable causes of poor quality. The diagram is called a fishbone because it looks like the bones of a fish. It was invented in 1943 by Kaoru Ishikawa and is sometimes called an *Ishikawa diagram.* The head of the fish is the effect—the quality problem. The bones leading from the spine are the possible causes of the problems. The diagram is drawn so that the spine of the fish connects the head to the possible causes of the problem. Each of the possible causes can then have smaller bones that address specific issues that relate to each cause. The advantages of using a fishbone diagram are several. For one, it permits a rigorous analysis of possible problem sources. Without it, the approach might be hit or miss depending on individual expertise. Also, it fosters "brainstorming" and gives the big picture as to possible causes or influencing factors. By recursively recoloring the diagram, one can obtain a clear indication of areas where further investigation resolution (test) efforts are needed and should be focused. Even after the problem is resolved, areas of weakness in the link design remain highlighted and could be rectified in the future. This method is economical of time and can be pursued without "going over the same ground over and over again" (Skjei, 2005).

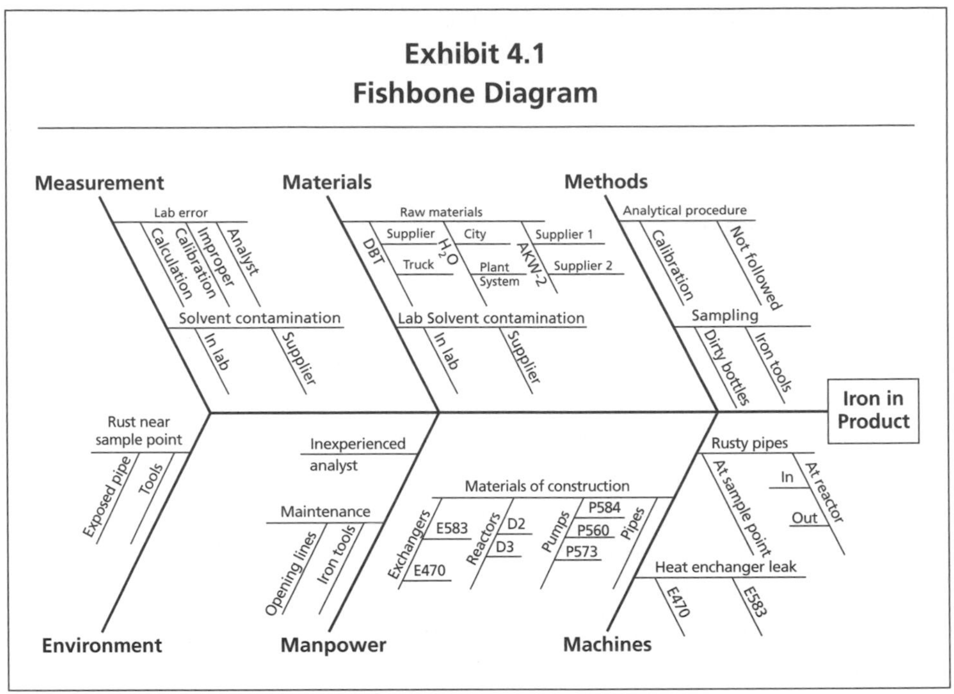


**Exhibit 4.1**
**Fishbone Diagram**

## EFFECTIVE TEST AND QUIZ DEVELOPMENT

Most often, instructors develop their own test questions or use those that have been provided as an accompaniment to the textbook in use for a course. These may not be the most effective means by which to develop test items, however. Weimer (2002) suggests a series of activities that can enhance the learning potential of an exam in addition to making all exams open-book, take-home exams. These suggestions, which can be applied easily in the online environment, are as follows:

- Include short activities in the course, such as practice tests or self-quizzes, that promote review of learning.
- Ask students to summarize course content on a regular basis as part of regular, ongoing online discussion. The One-Sentence Paper or the Critical Incident Questionnaire adapted for online use would serve this purpose.
- Ask students to generate and submit one potential test question for each content module and use these to create or augment a test bank for the course.

Case (2008) notes that most often test questions are developed by an individual instructor and thus represent the instructor's interpretation of the content.

Consequently, he recommends the use of collaborative teams made up of subject matter experts and staff skilled in psychometrics and assessment. Test items that do not appear to be effective, once the exam is delivered, should be reviewed and revised.

The following are some guidelines for effective construction of tests and quizzes for online delivery.

### Validity

- Items are written clearly and are understandable.
- Content directly matches learning outcomes or unit objectives or both.
- Items have appropriate weight to the final score.
- Level of thinking required, based on Bloom's Taxonomy, directly matches learning outcomes or objectives or both.
- Range of items is wide enough to represent learning outcomes.

### Reliability

- Instructions are clear.
- Time limits are reasonable and realistic.
- Test is password protected.
- Vocabulary used is consistent with that presented in course materials.
- Test layout is clear and consistent throughout.
- Make-up exams, if offered, are similar to the original exam.
- Randomization of items is used to create an individual test for each learner.

The following example is part of a lesson that includes self-testing as a means of ongoing formative assessment. It was developed by Laila Bicksler, an instructor at Delgado Community College, and also includes a discussion component.

## GOOD DAY, CLASS! WELCOME TO FACTORING 101!

In a normal Math 096 class, the materials here would be the second week of the factoring unit, approximately six weeks into the term. They have previously covered addition, subtraction, multiplication, and division of polynomials. In the first week of this unit, they computed basic square roots and cube roots. I'll take it for granted that you may have forgotten much of your previous mathematical knowledge. Therefore my presentation will be very basic.

*Instructor:* F. Laila Bicksler

*E-mail:* fmoham@dcc.edu

*Office:* (504) 361-6157

*This week's activities:* This week's work runs from Monday, December 18 at 12:01 AM until Saturday, December 23 at 11:59 PM.

Please complete the following steps in the order listed.

1. A review of prime factorization
2. The greatest common factor
3. Factoring by grouping
4. EZ trinomial factoring
5. Weekly review and wrap up

So let's get started! Don't forget to have some fun, and if you have any questions, send an e-SOS.

### Activity 1: A Review of Prime Factorization

Do you remember prime numbers? These are whole numbers bigger than 1 that have no factors other than 1 and themselves.

For example, the number 3 is prime because the only factors of 3 are 1 and 3.

Check out the first few prime numbers: 2, 3, 5, 7, 11, 13, 17, 19 . . .

***Just for fun, list the prime numbers from 1 through 100. (Answers to all these [***] problems are provided later.)

If a whole number bigger than 1 is not prime, then it is composite.

The number 6 is not prime because 6 = 1 * 6 and 6 = 2 * 3.

***Is the number 12 prime or composite? Why?

*Note:* Prime numbers and composite numbers are defined only for *whole numbers bigger than 1.*

*Listing all the factors of a number:* Take a number, such as 36. Beginning with 1, start dividing 36 by successive whole numbers. These numbers are the *prospective factors* of 36.

36 = 1 * 36

36 = 2 * 18

36 = 3 * 12

36 = 4 * 9

36 = 5 * 7.2 This does not divide evenly by 5, so 5 is not a factor of 36.

36 = 6 * 6

You can stop here because the factors are equal to each other.

The factors of 36 are 1, 2, 3, 4, 6, 9, 12, 18, 36.

***You try it! Find all the factors of 24.

Finally, even though there may be many sets of factors of a number, each number has only one prime factorization.

*Every number can be written uniquely as a product of primes.*

To find a number's prime factorization, make a factor tree:

144 Pick any two factors of 144.

12 * 12 Now check each factor to see if it is prime. If not, factor again.

4 * 3 * 4 * 3 Check all of the new factors to see if they are prime. If not, factor again.

2 * 2 * 3 * 2 * 2 * 3 Are they all prime yet?

The prime factorization of 144 is 2 * 2 * 3 * 2 * 2 * 3 or $2^4 * 3^2$.

***You try it! Find the prime factorization of 250.

**Answers to the *** problems**

1. List the prime numbers through 100.

   There are twenty-five:

   2, 3, 5, 7, 11, 13, 17, 19, 23, 29, 31, 37, 41, 43, 47, 53, 59, 61, 67, 71, 73, 79, 83, 89, 97

2. Is the number 12 prime or composite? Why?

   It is composite, because:

   12 = 12 * 1 and 12 = 2 * 6 and 12 = 3 * 4

3. You try it! Find all the factors of 24.

   24 = 1 * 24

   24 = 2 * 12

   24 = 3 * 8

   24 = 4 * 6

   24 = 5 * 4.8 Because this does not divide evenly, 5 is not a factor of 24.

   Stop here because 4.8 is less than 5.

   The factors of 24 are 1, 2, 3, 4, 6, 8, 12, and 24.

4. You try it! Find the prime factorization of 250.

   250

   125 * 2

   25 * 5 * 2

   5 * 5 * 5 * 2

   So the prime factorization of 250 is 5 * 5 * 5 * 2 = $5^3$ * 2

---

## YOUR ASSIGNMENT:

Are the following numbers prime or composite?

1. 13
2. 39
3. 87

Find all the factors of the following:

4. 60
5. 225
6. 136

Find the prime factorization of:

7. 24
8. 80

9. 125

10. 360

On the discussion board, in your own words, describe how to find the prime factorization of any number.

We are studying algebra. So why do you think that we reviewed prime factorization of numbers? Where do you think this is leading?

Tune in tomorrow for the answers.

### Activity 2A: Check your Work

Let's start by checking yesterday's work:

Are the following numbers prime or composite?

1. 13 Prime
2. 39 Composite 39 = 3 * 13 as well as 39 = 1 * 39
3. 87 Composite again! 87 = 3 * 29 as well as 87 = 1 * 87

Find all the factors of the following:

4. 60

   60 = 1 * 60

   60 = 2 * 30

   60 = 3 * 20

   60 = 4 * 15

   60 = 5 * 12

   60 = 6 * 10

   60 = 7 * 8.57 Seven does not go evenly into 60, so it is not a factor of 60.

   60 = 8 * 7.5 Eight does not go evenly into 60, so it is not a factor of 60.

You can stop here because the factor on the left is bigger than the one on the right.

The factors of 60 are 1, 2, 3, 4, 5, 6, 10, 12, 15, 20, 30, 60.

5. 225

   225 = 1 * 225

225 = 2 * 112.5 Two does not go evenly into 225, so it is not a factor of 225.

225 = 3 * 75

225 = 4 * 56.25 Four is not a factor of 225.

225 = 5 * 45

225 = 6 * 37.5 Six is not a factor of 225.

225 = 7 * 34.12 Seven is not a factor of 225.

225 = 8 * 28.125 Eight is not a factor of 225.

225 = 9 * 25

225 = 10 * 22.5 Ten is not a factor of 225.

225 = 11 * 20.45 Eleven is not a factor of 225.

225 = 12 * 18.75 Twelve is not a factor of 225.

225 = 13 * 17.03 Thirteen is not a factor of 225.

225 = 14 * 16.07 Fourteen is not a factor of 225.

225 = 15 * 15

You can stop here because both factors are equal.

The factors of 225 are 1, 3, 5, 9, 15, 25, 45, 75, 225.

6. 136

136 = 1 * 136

136 = 2 * 68

136 = 3 * 45.33 Three is not a factor of 136.

136 = 4 * 34

136 = 5 * 27.2 Five is not a factor of 136.

136 = 6 * 22.66 Six is not a factor of 136.

136 = 7 * 19.42 Seven is not a factor of 136.

136 = 8 * 17

136 = 9 * 15.11 Nine is not a factor of 136.

136 = 10 * 13.6 Ten is not a factor of 136.

136 = 11 * 12.36 Eleven is not a factor of 136.

136 = 12 * 11.33 Twelve is not a factor of 136.

You can stop here because the factor on the left is bigger than the one on the right.

The factors of 136 are 1, 2, 4, 8, 17, 34, 68, 136.

**Find the prime factorization of:**

7. 24

   24

   2 * 12

   2 * 2 * 6

   2 * 2 * 2 * 3

   24 = 2 * 2 * 2 * 3 or $2^3$ * 3

8. 80

   80

   2 * 40

   2 * 2 * 20

   2 * 2 * 2 * 10

   2 * 2 * 2 * 2 * 5

   80 = 2 * 2 * 2 * 2 * 5 or $2^4$ * 5

9. 125

   125

   5 * 25

   5 * 5 * 5

   125 = 5 * 5 * 5 or $5^3$

10. 360

    360

    2 * 180

    2 * 2 * 90

    2 * 2 * 2 * 45

    2 * 2 * 2 * 9 * 5

2 * 2 * 2 * 3 * 3 * 5

360 = 2 * 2 * 2 * 3 * 3 * 5 or $2^3 * 3^2 * 5$

**How did you do?**

All correct – You're a superstar!!! Keep up the great work!

Missed 1 or 2 – Good job! Did you figure out what your mistakes were? Can you avoid those same mistakes in the future?

Missed 3 or more – Let's go back and review the lesson. Figure out what you didn't understand. If you are still having problems, post your questions on the discussion board for all of us to explain it to you. Redo the homework lesson as well as the supplementary exercises. When you can complete the work comfortably, missing only one or two problems, go on to the next lesson.

---

## PORTFOLIOS

A portfolio is a collection of documents representative of an individual's best work over a period of time. Unlike summative assessments—such as tests—that measure performance on a given occasion, portfolios have the added benefit of measuring performance over time (Banta, 2003). This may include a variety of other kinds of process information (such as drafts of student work or students' self-assessment of their work). It is a purposeful, meaningful collection of student work that tells a story about the student's developmental growth, achievements, and progress over time. It is truly a learner-focused assessment in that it is up to the student to determine what should be included—what will best tell the story? The following are uses for portfolios.

**1. Growth Portfolio—Emphasizes the Process of Learning**

- To show growth or change over time
- To help develop process skills, such as self-evaluation and goal setting
- To identify strengths and weaknesses
- To track the development of one or more products or performances

**2. Showcase Portfolio—Emphasizes the Products of Learning**

- To showcase end-of-year/semester accomplishments

- To prepare a sample of best work for employment or college admission
- To showcase student perceptions of favorite, best, or most important work
- To communicate a student's current aptitudes to future teachers

**3. Evaluation or Proficiency Portfolio—Emphasizes Achievement of Outcomes or Competencies**

- To document achievement for grading purposes
- To document progress toward standards
- To place students appropriately

**4. Project Portfolio**

- To show the process for completing a project
- To document the various stages of the project and progress to completion
- To present the final project itself

**5. Professional Portfolio**

- To highlight important aspects of the professional career
- To contain a resume or CV and cover letter
- To contain any other products or artifacts deemed important and relevant to the career, such as papers written, professional presentations, and the like

*Portfolio Development.* Portfolios can be prepared in print format or online, through the creation of a website or the use of applications designed for e-portfolio development. Sewell, Marczac, and Horn (n.d.) present a discussion of portfolio development that highlights the main factors to be considered:

- What is the purpose that the portfolio will serve?
- What assessment criteria will be used to review it—that is, what is considered "successful completion" of the portfolio assignment?
- What sources of evidence should be used?
- How much evidence is needed to make good decisions and determinations?
- How does one make sense of the evidence that is collected?

## PORTFOLIOS AS ASSESSMENT

Portfolios can be used as assessments in several ways. Rubrics can be developed for assessment and grading purposes, and the following options for portfolio review can occur:

- The student can reflect on the portfolio and be given guiding questions to answer along with the rubric as a form of self-assessment.
- Portfolios can be presented to student peers, with feedback elicited and provided based on the rubric or other criteria.
- Portfolios can be presented to the instructor and serve as a basis for dialogue between the student and instructor regarding achievement of outcomes.
- Portfolios can be reviewed by a panel, generally at the end of a program of study or as a transition point in a program of study, to determine readiness to move on. The panel may include outside experts or others not associated with the academic program. In these cases, the criteria used need to be very specific and panelists should receive guidance on portfolio review.

*Rubrics for Portfolio Assessment.* The following are basic criteria that can be used to develop a rubric for portfolio assessment:

- *Relevance.* Portfolio components directly address learning objectives, outcomes, and competencies.
- *Scope.* All aspects of participation in the course are covered, including reading completed, papers written, tests and quizzes taken, participation in collaborative activities, participation in discussions, and so on.
- *Accuracy.* Course concepts, terms, principles, and the like are used correctly and with clarity throughout.
- *Coherence.* Elements are logically and structurally linked; ideas are interconnected and presented consistently throughout.
- *Depth.* A personal position is reflected and supported by analysis of material, reflections on learning, and the use of multiple quality resources and references.

The following is an example of a portfolio assignment we use in the capstone course of the Teaching in the Virtual Classroom program as a final assessment of competence.

## E-LEARNING AUTOBIOGRAPHY

Prepare and present a portfolio of knowledge and experience in online teaching and training in the form of an e-learning autobiography. This assignment is worth thirty points.

The e-learning autobiography is basically your story of your experiences with education in general and online teaching and learning in particular, with the stress being placed on what you've learned and what learning you have yet to do. It is our hope that it will be of sufficient interest to you that you will want to keep it for your own use.

Because it is your life, you must set the style and tone. You may include materials of interest, such as pictures or whatever you feel is appropriate. You may decide to create a graphic or website that illustrates your e-learning autobiography. You must decide for yourself how much you want to share, particularly because students will be sharing their e-learning autobiographies with one another. Some of our discussions in class will lead into the areas of the autobiography.

On the practical level, the e-learning autobiography is a look into the past and toward the future. It should be reflective and indicate directions, futures, hopes, goals, and objectives you have or are working toward. Thus the e-learning autobiography will assist in setting out any additional educational plans you might have. The e-learning autobiography is also a means by which to evaluate your own life experience in terms of how it relates to your past and future educational experiences.

*As a first step in the construction of your e-learning autobiography, write an introductory statement. Then answer the following questions:*

1. Formal education:

   In your past, which educational experiences were most meaningful? Which were least meaningful? Why? What have you learned about yourself as to the type of learner you are? In what types of situation(s) do you learn best?

2. People:

   What people have had the greatest impact on your life as models or mentors, or have helped you develop a sense of direction in life?

3. Significant incidents:

   What three (or more) significant incidents out of your past life experiences contributed most to the kind of person you are today, your personal sense of direction, where you see yourself going, and the values you hold? (For this answer, you may find it helpful to begin by writing a brief chronology of the events in your life.)

4. Informal learning, skills, and abilities:

   What other previous experience(s) have you had outside the formal classroom setting in which you have learned? What specific knowledge or skills have you gained through such experiences? (You may want to identify what you do or can do in your job.) What are your greatest talents, skills, and abilities? What skills, abilities, or knowledge do you most want to gain or improve on?

5. Goals:

   What are your future goals—personal, professional, and educational? What will you be doing (or what would you like to be doing) in five or ten years? What things stand in the way of your accomplishing these goals? What skills and knowledge do you still need to acquire in order to achieve your goals?

---

## REFLECTIVE ASSESSMENT AND SELF-ASSESSMENT

Depending on the level of the learners, criteria for self-assessment can be instructor developed, peer developed, or independently developed. Self-assessment generally works best with some guiding questions and can be used effectively for individual activities as well as overall performance in the course. The following are some guiding questions that can be used for self-assessments:

- Who was I as a learner before I entered this course?
- Have I changed? If so, how?
- How has my participation in this course changed my learning process or my view of myself as a learner?
- What have I gained (or not) by participating in this course?
- Have I learned anything new about the topic or myself?

- What suggestions do I have for future groups participating in this course or for the instructor of this course?
- Would I recommend this course to my friends and colleagues? Why or why not?
- How do I evaluate my own contributions to the course? What grade would I give myself? (Palloff & Pratt, 2003, pp. 177–178)

Brookfield (1995) suggests the concept of writing a letter to successors as a means by which a course can be evaluated. The questions presented could form the basis of such a letter and could then serve two purposes—it would provide a form of self-assessment while providing the instructor with summative feedback that can be applied to quality improvement in course development. We have found that when students provide this feedback in the form of a letter to prospective future students, it tends to lessen inhibitions around providing substantive feedback that can be useful in modifying the course.

*Reflective Assessment.* Another form of reflection that can be included in an online course as assessment is a reflective activity that encourages students to reflect on course concepts and apply them in a new way, thus creating a synthesis of thoughts and evidence of original thought. This reflective activity was contributed by Brian Trautman, who is developing online courses in Peace Studies.

*Instructor:* Brian J. Trautman, M.Ed.
*Institution:* Berkshire Community College
*Course:* PHL-Alternatives to Violence
*Term:* Spring 2008

## ASSIGNMENT #1 PERSONAL ESSAY: VIOLENCE, FEAR—AND PERSONAL EXPERIENCE

(10 points or 10% of your total course grade)

**Background:**

To reduce or eliminate violence in our personal lives, as well as in society, we must continue to grow our strategies to creatively address and manage violent situations. The violence we witness every day, either directly or indirectly, must be counteracted through a consciousness and culture of nonviolence. How can we avoid, prevent, and counter violence through a state of mind and behavior consistent with nonviolent principles and approaches? Why do we, both individually and as a society, tend to react to violence or the threat of violence in violent ways? What is the state of mind and behavior of those who have been victims of violence and of those who avoided or escaped violence? Why do fear and acts of counterviolence perpetuate violent thought and action? How can we discourage violence? How can we act positively and constructively toward violent situations, including those situations where the potential for violence exists? What individual experiences inform our understanding of, and our ability to effectively engage, the violence that is all around us?

## Expectations:

This activity will help you develop an increased awareness of, and an enhanced appreciation for, many problems and solutions in relation to threats of violence toward individuals and society. You will acquire knowledge and understanding of several theories and techniques for nonviolent conflict resolution. Through this activity, you will reveal personal connections with stories and examples from the book *Safe Passage on City Streets* by Dorothy T. Samuel (1991). You are expected to develop a clear understanding of the content and message of the book, of how it speaks to a personal experience, and of how you can use approaches described in the book to counter violence through nonviolent means.

## Learning Outcomes:

- Learners will develop an understanding and appreciation for nonviolent approaches to violent thought and behavior.
- Learners will reflect on and share personal experiences about how the fear of violence or the act of counterviolence was used to end a violent situation.
- Learners will acquire knowledge about effective approaches to avoid, prevent, and counter violence through creative, nonviolent alternatives.

- Learners will enhance their ability to analyze pathways to violence and nonviolence.
- Learners will grow in their awareness and critical perception of the relationship between fear and violence.
- Learners will demonstrate an understanding of the content and message of the book *Safe Passage* through a critique of how the book speaks to personal experiences dealing with violence and to nonviolent methods of countering violence in the future.

## THE ASSIGNMENT:

### Violence, Fear—and Personal Experience
### *Safe Passage on City Streets* by Dorothy T. Samuel

**Step 1:** Read the entire book.

**Step 2:** As you read the book, create an outline of major points and examples that you feel speak to one or more of your personal experiences with the types of violence discussed. Think about (and write down for future reference) how the positive approaches to violence described in the book may have, in retrospect, facilitated a change in outcome in your example, perhaps through a specific act that could have helped you avoid, prevent, or counter the violence through nonviolent means. Make sure you also write down the approaches learned from the book that you believe may help you counter violence or the threat of violence in some present situation or some future hypothetical circumstance.

**Step 3:** After reading the book, continue to think about an event in your personal life or one you observed elsewhere that has some similarity to a confrontation described in the book. Use the outline you created as a guide and write a response (three to five pages) in essay format to the following:

- Describe the event. Was the outcome similar to the one used in the reading? Was the approach used (by you or by participants or observers) to resolve the confrontation similar to the one used in the reading?

- Evaluate any differences or similarities in approaches and results between the confrontation discussed in the book and the personal or other event chosen.
- Describe some approaches from the book that you feel may help you avoid, prevent, and counter violence through nonviolent means in the future. (*Note:* If you have no experience to write about, find an illustrative example in a newspaper or periodical and use that as the basis for your answer.)

Your grade will be based on the following scoring rubric:

**Response Rubric for Reflective Essay**

**9–10 A Nine- to Ten-Point Response:**

- Is in complete, well-written sentences that clearly address all aspects of the assignment questions
- Demonstrates an understanding of both stated and unstated meanings of the text and how they relate to the chosen personal event
- Offers ideas supported with many specific examples from the text
- Extends response by
  - Making connections to multiple events (such as global), beyond personal events
  - Drawing conclusions, generalizing, or summarizing
  - Noting the author's style or point of view
- Is reflective and purposeful and shows a considerable amount of critical thought and thoroughness

7–8 **A Seven- to Eight-Point Response:**

- Is in complete, well-written sentences that clearly address all aspects of the assignment questions in the response
- Demonstrates an understanding of both stated and unstated meanings of the text and how they relate to the chosen personal event
- Supports ideas with several specific examples from the text
- May extend response by
  - Making connections to at least one event beyond personal events (such as a global event)
  - Drawing conclusions, generalizing, or summarizing
  - Noting the author's style or point of view
- Is purposeful and shows adequate thought and effort

5–6 **A Five- to Six-Point Response:**

- Is in complete sentences that reflect minimal aspects of each question in the response
- Demonstrates an understanding of stated meanings of the text and how they relate to the chosen personal event
- Provides several descriptive statements to illustrate understanding
- May support ideas with examples from the text
- Shows casual thought and effort

3–4 **A Three- to Four-Point Response:**

- Is in complete sentences, but may be missing some aspects of the questions in the response
- Demonstrates an understanding of stated meanings of the text and how they relate to the chosen personal event
- Provides few descriptive statements to illustrate understanding
- Does not support ideas with examples from the text
- Shows little thought and minimal effort

1–2 **A One- to Two-Point Response:**

- May be in complete sentences, but is missing or misinterpreting many aspects of the questions in the response
- Is general and shows uncertain understanding of stated meanings
- Provides either no details or vague explanations to illustrate understanding
- Does not support ideas with examples from the text
- Shows very little thought and insufficient effort

*Source:* Rubric template adapted from
www.kyrene.org/schools/brisas/sunda/documents/RRubric.htm.

### Post-Assignment Activity:

You will be asked to share details from your papers with peers in small groups. A class discussion will follow to communicate any concluding reflections and feedback.

Another example of a reflective assessment that includes a collaborative component was contributed by Mark Burris, a philosophy instructor at the community college level.

## LESSON PLAN FOR MODULE 1: WHAT IS PHILOSOPHY ALL ABOUT?

*Instructor:* Mark Burris

### Objectives for Module 1

When you complete this module, you should be able to

1. Describe Plato's Allegory of the Cave
2. Relate Plato's Allegory to three major areas of philosophy
3. Reflect on the meaning of philosophy and its practical application to life

### Overview

One of the most important documents in the history of philosophy and one of the ones most enjoyed by students is Plato's Allegory of the Cave. Plato tells this story to illustrate his view of the various aspects of philosophy. But there is far more to this story than that!

We will use this story to introduce three major areas of philosophy and to answer the question, "What is philosophy and why should I care?"

There are four assignments in Module 1 related to this story. Each assignment will be graded according to the grading chart indicated in each assignment (all grading charts appear after the assignment descriptions). You will have one week to complete each assignment.

### Assignment 1. Metaphysics: Appearance Versus Reality

(Individual discussion topic; 15 points possible based on the Discussion Grading Chart.)

Click on the preceding link and read the story a couple of times. The conversation is a little strange by our modern standards, so you'll probably understand it better after reading it twice.

Then, using your computer, compose a brief description of the scene (one or two paragraphs) in your own words.

Then, in the same document, answer the following questions: What are the different ways that Plato's story distinguishes appearance from reality? What are the symbols or metaphors that he uses to make this distinction? Are there different realities expressed in this story or only one reality with several levels of appearances?

Finally, post the contents of your document to the discussion board and reply to at least two other student postings. Discussion posting will be evaluated according to the grading chart criteria mentioned earlier.

### Assignment 2. Epistemology: Knowledge Versus Opinion

(Paired discussion and collaborative presentation; 30 points possible based on the Group Presentation Rubric.)

Based on the postings in Assignment 1, choose a partner with whom you agree and prepare a collaborative presentation about Plato's distinction between knowledge and opinion.

Here are some questions to consider, but feel free to add your own. What does the word *shadows* illustrate in Plato's story? What does Plato use to illustrate knowledge? How do the prisoners define *knowledge*? Why does the guide in the story drag the released prisoner to the mouth of the cave, and what does this imply about gaining knowledge? Which is more pleasant—knowledge or opinion?

Individual students will then comment on at least two pair presentations. Comments will be evaluated based on the grading chart criteria mentioned earlier.

### Assignment 3. Ethics: Duty Versus Pleasure

(Paired discussion and collaborative presentation; 30 points possible based on the Group Presentation Rubric.)

Stay in your pair and join another pair, making one group of four students.

Notice in the story that Plato does not allow the philosophers to live outside of the cave, but allows them to go outside only periodically.

Discuss within your group and prepare to defend whether that is an effective life strategy and in what ways this scene illustrates our relationship to society.

### Assignment 4. Reflection: Living Inside Versus Living Outside of the Cave

(Individual discussion topic; 15 points possible based on the Discussion Grading Chart.)

Think about your own life. Briefly describe a time when you sincerely thought that something was correct or right but later discovered that you were mistaken.

Did you feel as if a fog had been lifted and that you could now see things more clearly? Or did you feel as if you had been naive, and perhaps a little foolish; that is to say, did you feel more happy afterward or did you feel pain? How do these feelings compare to those experienced by the released prisoner in Plato's story?

What other insights did you experience while discussing Plato's Allegory?

Now to the question that started this conversation. Based on Plato's Allegory and the discussion we've had so far, what is your response to the question, "What is philosophy and why should I care?"

### Discussion Grading Chart

| 15 Points possible | 0 Points | 1 Point | 3 Points | 4 Points | 5 Points |
|---|---|---|---|---|---|
| **Content** | Discussion questions not addressed; resources or readings not mentioned. | Some discussion questions are addressed; resources or readings are mentioned but not related to topic. | Discussion questions are addressed; resources or readings are cited and related to topic. | Previous level, plus incorporates readings and resources into own experiences. | Previous level, plus offers resources related to topic that are not found in the textbook or assigned readings. |

| 15 Points possible | 0 Points | 1 Point | 3 Points | 4 Points | 5 Points |
|---|---|---|---|---|---|
| **Language** | Thought processes are incomplete. Postings contain spelling *and* grammar errors. | Thought processes are complete. Postings contain spelling *or* grammar errors. | Thought processes are complete. Postings contain no spelling or grammar errors. | Previous level, plus arguments are clear, concise, and cogent; the post is timely; and relevant references are cited. | Previous level, plus incorporates previous learning into relevant topic or topics. |
| **Response** | Posts are limited (for example, "I agree with . . ." without explanation or discussion); posts are late without notice. | Posts are on time but brief and provide only a superficial discussion of the assigned topic. | Posts are on time and contain extended discussion relevant to topic. | Previous level, plus responses relate theory to practical or personal application, or both. | Previous level, plus posts are insightful and combine multiple ideas related to the topic. |

## Group Presentation Rubric

30 points possible

**Rubric for Individual Performance on a Team (15 points possible)**

| Objectives | Low Performance 1 point | Below Average 2 points | At or Above Average 3 points | Exemplary Performance 5 points |
|---|---|---|---|---|
| **Teamwork** | Only one person presented. Unclear team roles. | Clear team roles but unequal contributions. | Clear roles, equal contributions. | Clear roles, balanced contributions, good transitions between presenters. |
| **Presentation Style and Delivery** | No introduction or overview. Poor style (disorganized, difficult to follow). Went above or below page limits. | Appropriate introduction to topic but opinions expressed inadequately or vaguely. Barely met page limits. | Generally good delivery, presents arguments or opinions in a convincing manner. | Excellent style, involving matching written and nonverbal styles (graphics). Creative and imaginative. |

(*Continued*)

| Objectives | Low Performance 1 point | Below Average 2 points | At or Above Average 3 points | Exemplary Performance 5 points |
|---|---|---|---|---|
| **Information/ Content** | Does not have a grasp of information; opinions stated but not supported by information. For second presentation: no discussion on search tools chosen to fulfill the task. Did not rank websites according to reliability. | Incorporates few facts or little information to support ideas or opinions. For second presentation: search engines or other tools only cursorily mentioned. Gave a brief listing of rankings. | Demonstrates grasp of knowledge. Incorporates ample hints or strategies. For second presentation: mentioned the specific search tools used and why. Gave a full listing of rankings. | Complete and accurate presentation of important, related strategies or facts. Good use of technical or subject vocabulary. For second presentation: provided several reasons for using selected databases or search engines. Provided reasons for the ranking of topic websites. |

**Rubric for Individual Performance on a Team (15 points possible)**

| | Unacceptable: 0 points | Needs Improvement: 1 point | Accomplished: 2 points | Exemplary: 3 points |
|---|---|---|---|---|
| **General Communication** | Often is publicly critical of the project or the work of other members of the group. Fails to communicate a sense of teamwork in e-mail or discussion postings. | Occasionally is publicly critical of the project or the work or other members of the group. Most of the time communicates a sense of teamwork in e-mail or discussion postings. | Rarely is publicly critical of the project or the work of others. Often communicates a sense of teamwork in e-mail or discussion postings. | Never is publicly critical of the project or the work of others. Always communicates a sense of teamwork in e-mail or discussion postings. |

| | Unacceptable: 0 points | Needs Improvement: 1 point | Accomplished: 2 points | Exemplary: 3 points |
|---|---|---|---|---|
| **Working with Others** | Rarely listens to, shares with, or supports the efforts of others. Often is not a good team player. | Often listens to, shares with, or supports the efforts of others, but sometimes is not a good team player. | Usually listens to, shares with, or supports the efforts of others. Does not cause "waves" in the group. | Always listens to, shares with, or supports the efforts of others. Tries to keep people working well together. |
| **Collaboration** | Rarely provides useful ideas when participating in the group and in classroom discussion. May refuse to participate. | Sometimes provides useful ideas when participating in the group and in classroom discussion. | Usually provides useful ideas when participating in the group and in classroom discussion. A strong group member who tries hard. | Routinely provides useful ideas when participating in the group and in classroom discussion. A definite leader who contributes a lot of effort. |
| **Preparedness** | Often forgets needed materials or is rarely ready to get to work. | Almost always brings needed materials but sometimes needs to settle down and get to work. | Almost always brings needed materials. | Brings needed materials to class and is always ready to work. |
| **Focus on Task and Time Management** | Rarely focuses on the task and what needs to be done, and does not respect deadlines. Lets others do the work. Group has to adjust deadlines or work responsibilities because of this person's inadequate time management and lack of collaboration. | Focuses on the task and what needs to be done some of the time. Other group members must sometimes nag, prod, and remind to keep this person on task. Tends to procrastinate, but finally always gets things done by the deadlines. | Focuses on the task and what needs to be done most of the time and uses time well throughout the project. Other group members can count on this person. However, may have procrastinated on one thing or another. | Consistently stays focused on the task and what needs to be done. Very self-directed. Uses time well throughout the project to ensure things get done on time. Does not procrastinate. |

## COLLABORATIVE PEER ASSESSMENT

After collaborative activity, peer assessment can be used to debrief both the process and the outcome. Peer assessments can be in the form of a private e-mail to the instructor, including both self-assessment and assessment of all other members of the group and team, and can include suggested grades or simply be in narrative form. The following are some guidelines for collaborative assessment:

- Collaborative activities are best assessed collaboratively!
- The information gathered through collaborative assessment should not be given less emphasis than the information gathered through direct observation or evaluation by the instructor.

When assessing collaborative activities collaboratively, the instructor should:

- Give a group grade for the final product
- Have group members assess themselves and each group member privately through e-mail
- Have group members discuss and evaluate the process on the discussion board

Veto power regarding grades remains with the instructor if there are discrepancies between individual and group assessments. We generally recommend the use of *both* group grades and individual grades for collaborative work. The final product of the group is assessed based on specific criteria and a rubric, and individuals receive a grade based on the level of their participation as determined by self-assessment and peer assessment. The following form can be used for assessment of collaborative activities:

| **Collaboration Factors** | **Strongly Agree 1** | **Somewhat Agree 2** | **Neither Agree nor Disagree 3** | **Somewhat Disagree 4** | **Strongly Disagree 5** |
|---|---|---|---|---|---|
| We established common goals. | | | | | |
| We communicated well as a team. | | | | | |
| We chose a leader without difficulty. | | | | | |
| We assigned roles without difficulty. | | | | | |
| Everyone contributed equally to the process. | | | | | |

| Collaboration Factors | Strongly Agree 1 | Somewhat Agree 2 | Neither Agree nor Disagree 3 | Somewhat Disagree 4 | Strongly Disagree 5 |
|---|---|---|---|---|---|
| Everyone contributed equally to the final product. | | | | | |
| We had adequate time and resources to complete our task. | | | | | |
| I was satisfied with the way we worked together. | | | | | |
| I was satisfied with the final outcome. | | | | | |
| I feel that I learned from this activity. | | | | | |

The following is an example of a fishbowl activity in an elementary statistics course offered at Jamestown Community College that incorporates collaborative assessment techniques.

## ELEMENTARY STATISTICS

*Instructor:* Stephanie Zwyghuizen

### Welcome to Statistics!

#### Content-based objectives

- To know and be able to use the vocabulary and notation associated with sampling and experimental design at the *elementary level*
- To apply what we have learned about various sampling methods, sampling biases, and experimental design considerations to a real-life situation

#### Additional Objectives

- To begin building a learning community (see http://www-users.cs.york.ac.uk/~adisornn/research.htm)
- To place these topics in a real-world context that allows statistics to cross over into disciplines outside of mathematics (see http://elrond.scam.ecu.edu.au/oliver/2002/Reeves.pdf, p. 3)

**Scoring** Your final score for homework 1 will be based on the following:

| | |
|---|---|
| Participation in the team ice-breaker (in Module 0) | 5 points |
| Fishbowl participation (section follows) | 10 points |
| Final collaborative post for your team's fishbowl | 10 points |
| Response to the other team's fishbowl (section follows) | 5 points |
| Self-assessment or summary of your learning and contributions for the week | 10 points |
| Evaluation of your teammates | 5 points |
| Survey on this week's activity | 5 points |
| Total | 50 points |

Please see the course schedule for specific due dates.

### Instructions for Fishbowl Participation

During the week, you are to provide a minimum of two substantive posts to your team's fishbowl. A post such as "Good idea" or "I agree with Bob" is not considered substantive. Instead, your post should demonstrate something you learned from this week's resources (the mini-lectures on 1.1–1.5, our textbook and the practice exercises from the textbook, other statistics textbooks, any websites that have been provided, and so on) or somehow add to your team's discussion.

### Instructions for Final Collaborative Post

At the end of the week, when you have sorted out all of the details, the team leader is to create a final post that summarizes your team's survey or experiment design. *Each* team member's score for this post will be based not only on the content and quality of the final post but also on that member's evaluation by teammates.

### Instructions for Response to Other Team's Fishbowl

Over the weekend, post a substantive response to the other team's fishbowl discussion. This response can highlight some of the things you learned from the other team's discussion, it can critique the other team's design, and it can also pose questions for the other team.

## Instructions for Self-Assessment and Evaluation of Teammates

Over the weekend, you will submit a private self-assessment that gives a brief summary of what you learned and describes your contribution to your team. You will also evaluate the performance of your teammates.

## Instructions for Survey

Because this activity is new for me too, I will need some feedback about what went well and what needs to be improved. Please take the survey after you have completed all of the other activities for this chapter.

## Teammate Evaluation

You will earn 5 points for completing this evaluation.

*Your answers will remain confidential.*

1. Because the groups for this assignment were rather large, it might be difficult for you to gauge the performance of each group member. However, if there were any group members who caused problems (by rudeness, lack of participation, consistently presenting careless or low-quality work, and the like), I need to know. Please list the names of any such members. If you were satisfied with everyone's performance, please state that.
2. If you listed names in your answer to question 1, please evaluate those students according to the following grid (*Engaging the Online Learner,* Conrad & Donaldson, 2004, p. 30). There is a table for you to fill in below the grid.

| | *Points* | | | |
|---|---|---|---|---|
| ***Criteria*** | **0** | **1** | **2** | **3** |
| Cooperation | Did not listen to and did not value the opinions of others | Listened to but did not value the opinion of others, or valued the opinions of others but did not listen to them | Actively listened to, but it was not evident that he or she valued, the opinion of others | Actively listened to and valued the opinions of others |

(*Continued*)

| Criteria | Points 0 | 1 | 2 | 3 |
|---|---|---|---|---|
| Contribution | Did not contribute to the completion of the project | Contributed to the project, but work was inferior or inadequate | Contributed to the completion of the project with adequate work | Contributed to the completion of the project and submitted high-quality work |
| Participation | Did not participate in the group | Occasionally participated in the group | Often participated in the group | Consistently participated in the group |

**Evaluation**

| **Team Member** | **Score for Cooperation** | **Score for Contribution** | **Score for Participation** | **Total Score (out of 9 points possible)** |
|---|---|---|---|---|
| | | | | |

3. Do you have any additional comments you would like to make about your team?

*Self-assessment:* These questions are very open ended. Because they are meant to help you analyze your own learning and your own contributions to the course, there are no right or wrong answers. To earn the 10 points for this part of the assignment, you need only to provide thoughtful, carefully written paragraphs that clearly address the question being asked.

1. Write one or two paragraphs describing or explaining the most important thing you learned this week about designing surveys.
2. Write one or two paragraphs describing or explaining the most important thing you learned this week about designing experiments.

3. Write one or two paragraphs describing your reactions or observations about working in a group in an online environment.
4. Using the grid provided for evaluating a team member's performance, evaluate your own performance in the group and explain why you chose those ratings.

---

## THE USE OF WIKIS AND BLOGS IN ASSESSMENT

Blogs and wikis are means by which knowledge can be socially constructed in an online course. Blogs are online web logs; wikis are collaboratively created web pages. Here are some of the differences and similarities between them:

- With blogs, material is posted as a journal in chronological fashion, and there is no editing of content by another—others are free to add comments and to respond to the blog, but not to alter it in any way. Wikis, on the other hand, allow for editing of material by those in the group.
- Both blogs and wikis are likely to contain links to outside resources.
- Blogs are most often individually created but can be team projects; wikis are almost always team projects.
- Blogs are only sometimes assessed, and generally the assessments address their creation rather than their content.
- Assessment of blogs can involve the use of outside experts, who also engage in blogging in the same blog spot.
- Wikis are assessed as a collaborative activity, generally involving the use of a rubric.
- Blogs and wikis can be created within course management systems and kept password protected or can be created on sites on the Internet designated for that purpose. When blogs and wikis are created in public spaces, it becomes easier to involve outside experts for the review of content as part of the assessment process.

The following activity involving the use of a wiki was created by Steve Keithley, director of instructional media services for the Santa Barbara Education Office. The activity includes a rubric for assessment purposes.

## EVALUATION OF AMERICAN PUBLIC SCHOOLS' EDUCATIONAL TECHNOLOGY

### Objective:

To critically evaluate the concept of digital resources in American public schools in light of recent ideas about changing demographics and a global economy. To make recommendations for improving the use of technology in public schools, keeping in mind the limited funds schools have.

### Resources:

Institute of Education Sciences U.S. Department of Education Report: Internet Access in U.S. Public Schools and Classrooms: 1994–2003. Sections: "Background" and "Selected Findings." Retrieved August 4, 2007 from http://nces.ed.gov/surveys/frss/publications/2005015/

"Shift Happens." www.youtube.com/watch?v=ljbl-363A2Q

### Tasks:

**Day 1:**

1. Form two groups of two or three students and give your group a name. Read the suggested article sections "Background" and "Selected Findings," then watch the video.
2. As a team, discuss (in this forum, by adding a new discussion topic) the relationship between what was viewed in the film clip and what you read in the article, then write a brief Summary of Suggestions for how schools might respond to the ideas posed in both the clip and the article.

**Day 2:**

1. Submit the Summary of Suggestions to the whole-class wiki(http://edu502.wikispaces.com/).
2. As a team, choose another team's Summary and evaluate the feasibility of the suggestions posed by the group you've chosen.

**Day 3:**

Carefully consider the other team's evaluation of your Summary and respond to their evaluation.

**Day 4:**

*Self-reflection:* Each student will formulate a personal statement on his or her values about the issue of technology in public schools. This will be a single paragraph and submitted in the discussion forum, *not* the wiki.

## Evaluation:

The quality of analysis and evaluation of the group's review of the other team's Summary of Suggestions and level of digital equity will determine the group's grade. All members of the group will share the same grade. The following rubric will be used.

| | Insufficient (1) | Competent (2) | Proficient (3) | Exemplary (4) | Score |
|---|---|---|---|---|---|
| Summary of Suggestions from article and film | Summary of Suggestions does not summarize the video or reading. Does not address issues the materials evoke. | Summary of Suggestions covers some points but misses some key elements. | Summary of Suggestions thoroughly covers key components of the video and reading. Considers some budgetary and equity issues. | Summary of Suggestions thoroughly covers several issues in educational technology. Considers budgetary, equity, and other issues. | |
| Evaluation of other team's Summary of Suggestions | Does not evaluate the other team's work. | Evaluations are basic and do not consider or discuss the other team's Summary in detail. | Evaluation considers multiple factors in detail and makes suggestions for improvement. | Evaluation is thorough and includes specific feedback on each suggestion made by the other group. Considers a wide variety of factors when making additional feedback. | |

Tina Montemer, who teaches technology integration, created the following activity that teaches the creation and use of blogs for teachers.

*Important:* Please be sure to read the syllabus, as it contains the overall course objectives, expectations for the class, required readings, and other pertinent information.

### Week 1 Lesson Plan

The activities for this first week will lay the foundation for the rest of the semester.

This week's objectives:

- To introduce ourselves and get to know each other
- To become familiar with the discussion board
- To become familiar with social networking and how it is used in today's classrooms
- To begin a personal learning journal by creating a personal blog

**Task 1:** Read the following article and post a summary reflection in the lesson folder.

> How To: Use Social-Networking Technology for Learning, Edutopia, April 2007. www.edutopia.org/how-use-social-networking-technology

**Task 2:** Read the article at the following link.

> Edublogs We Love: Ten Top Stops for Internet Interaction, Edutopia, September 2007. www.edutopia.org/whats-next-2007-best-blogs

Visit the blogs presented in the article.

Select one or two that you find interesting and helpful. Post a comment on why you selected them.

**Task 3:** Read the article at the following link.

> Digital Discussion: Take Your Class to the Internet,
> Edutopia, September 2007.
> www.edutopia.org/whats-next-2007-classroom-blog-setup

You are to create a personal blog that will serve as your learning journal for this class. Be creative and let the blog speak to your personality.

Go to https://www.blogger.com/start

Setting up a blog takes only a few minutes. Just follow the instructions (create an account, and choose a name and template).

Make sure you complete your profile (About Me) and include information about yourself and any other information you may want to share with the class.

For a sample of a personal blog, visit my personal blog at: http://mmthlvr.blogspot.com/

After you have finished creating your blog, post a summary of what you've learned this week in the lesson folder. Be sure to include your blog address so others can visit.

Visit two blogs from the class and post a comment on each.

If you have trouble with Task 3, seek the help of one of the Digital Natives (or you can e-mail me).

**Additional Resources:**

Richardson, W. (2006). Blogs, Wikis, Podcasts, and Other Powerful Web Tools for Classrooms. Corwin Press.

Prensky, M. Listen to the Natives. *Educational Leadership,* December 2005/January 2006, 63(4). www.ascd.org/cms/objectlib/ascdframeset/index.cfm?publication=www.ascd.org/authors/ed_lead/el200512_prensky.html

Prensky, M. (2001). Digital Natives, Digital Immigrants. www.marcprensky.com/writing/Prensky%20-%20Digital%20Natives,%20Digital%20Immigrants%20-%20Part1.pdf

---

## EFFECTIVE ONLINE COURSE EVALUATION

The following is a sample of a course evaluation that we use in our Teaching in the Virtual Classroom program. This online form is completed anonymously and the results are computer-aggregated. The reader will note that this evaluation was built on the concepts promoted by Stephen Brookfield (1995) and incorporates pieces of the Critical Incident Questionnaire.

## COURSE EVALUATION: TEACHING IN THE VIRTUAL CLASSROOM PROGRAM

Your feedback is important to us! Thank you for completing this survey!

1. Please select the course to evaluate. A set of course names follows.
2. Please select the cohort to which you belong. A set of class cohorts follows.

How much do you agree or disagree with the following statements?

| | Not Applicable | Strongly Disagree | Disagree | Agree | Strongly Agree |
|---|---|---|---|---|---|
| 3. The course is well organized. | | | | | |
| 4. Course readings are relevant to course objectives. | | | | | |
| 5. Course assignments are relevant to course objectives. | | | | | |
| 6. In this course, different instructional approaches are used. | | | | | |

Please rate the following elements:

| | Not Applicable | Needs Improvement | Average | Above Average | Excellent |
|---|---|---|---|---|---|
| 7. Quality of online feedback by colleagues | | | | | |
| 8. Quality of interaction with instructors | | | | | |
| 9. Quality of instructor responsiveness | | | | | |

10. Do you have any additional comments on items 3 through 9?
11. How did the course add value to your professional or personal learning goals?
12. What most helped you to take responsibility for your learning in this class?
13. What most prevented you from taking responsibility for your learning in this class?
14. What area of your development as a learner do you most need to work on as a result of taking this class?
15. Overall, in which moments in the course were you the most engaged, excited, and involved as a learner?
16. Overall, in which moments in the course were you the most distanced, disengaged, and uninvolved as a learner?
17. What would you most like to say about your experiences as a learner in this course?
18. What piece of advice would you most like to give to the instructor(s) on how to facilitate this course in the future or to future learners who take this course?
19. Please share any other comments you may have.

---

## EFFECTIVE FACULTY EVALUATION

The following checklist can be used by administrators in the evaluation of online faculty, drawing from a number of sources that have created rubrics for course design, development, and facilitation, along with our own experience in designing and facilitating online courses. We have separated the functions into course design and course facilitation, given that these are the two main categories of faculty function. In cases where the faculty member who is facilitating the course has written the course, both checklists can be used. If the instructor is facilitating a course written by another, the facilitation checklist can be used in isolation. Finally, the checklists could be developed into rubrics. The items in the checklist represent exemplary performance; they could be evaluated using a numeric scale or placed in a grid with approximations of developmental performance established to measure growth. The following are the exemplary characteristics of faculty performance.

**Course Design**

- All competencies are clearly stated and written using action verbs that promote higher-order thinking skills and communicate what learners will be able to do as a result of the learning experience.
- All competencies are observable and measurable—the instructor and learner will be able to see a product, a process, or both on completion of the learning experience, and its quality is measurable.
- All competencies clearly represent knowledge, skills, or attitudes or values that the learner would use in applying course knowledge to real-world situations.
- Course content, outcomes, practice, and assessment are consistent, and the relationships among them are clear.
- Outcomes are linked to program competencies or professional standards when applicable.
- Material is chunked, meaning that it is divided into appropriate categories, units, lessons, and so on, and it contains learning strategies that involve both recall and application.
- Lesson or unit design includes clear learning objectives, motivational techniques, and application activities, including discussion questions, and assessments that align with the material and the objectives for the unit.
- In addition to overall expectations and directions, each activity or assignment clearly indicates what students need to do, how and where they should submit results, and so on.
- Assessment methods are designed so as to measure progress toward program competencies and course outcomes, and there is strong alignment between assessment and outcomes.
- Course resources are current and are fully accessible to all students. Instructions are available on the site directing those with disabilities on how to access all course resources.

**Course Facilitation**

- The instructor has posted course requirements clearly stating that students are required to interact with each other and with the instructor, a designated timeframe for the interaction is stated, directions for how to participate in the interaction are provided, standards for the quality or expectations of the interaction are set, and the outcomes of those interactions are noted (that is, students receive points or a grade for the interaction).
- The instructor has made clear effort to establish a learning community among students in the course through the use of introductions, bios, and ice-breaker activities, the creation of a social space or café area in the course, promotion of informal communication, appropriate use of humor, and other appropriate efforts to personalize and humanize the course.
- Students are required to respond to discussion questions about the content of each unit or somehow apply what was learned for all learning objectives in the unit. Multiple methods of interaction are available and utilized (such as discussion board, e-mail, chat, virtual classroom technology). The instructor responds to student postings strategically, allowing for extension and deepening of the exploration of content.
- Guidelines provided by the instructor at the start of the course state that the instructor will provide feedback within a designated timeframe, a clear description of how the task of providing feedback will be accomplished (how the student will receive the feedback—e-mail, discussion board, and so on), and the specific types of feedback that will be submitted—for example, feedback on assignments and on class participation—and the instructor holds to those guidelines.
- Learning activities are developed that support instructor-to-student interaction (instructor participates in discussion with students via a discussion board or virtual chat room) and student-to-content interaction (such as responses to discussion questions regarding the content), and student-to-student interaction is promoted, supported, and required as part of the course through collaborative projects, group assignments, discussion board, or virtual chat assignments.
- Assessment of student learning is established and is given in a time period that supports the student's learning, soon after learning activities have taken place.

- Assessments are designed so that they are responsive to the needs of the individual learner; for example, alternative measures may be taken for students with special needs; assessments are designed to reflect the student population and are varied enough that they meet the needs of diverse learning styles; assessments involve student choice.
- Students' achievement of stated learning outcomes is documented and provided to the students as feedback on their learning activities and assessments; informal as well as formal feedback are provided by the instructor to the students and encouraged from student to student.
- A rubric is used for all gradable activities that illustrates what achievement will look like and requires both student and instructor input.
- The instructor offers multiple opportunities for students to give feedback on course content and the technology in use, and uses the feedback to make course adjustments as necessary.

## Portfolio Review for Online Faculty

The following document was designed collaboratively by the faculty of the Organization Management and Development program at Fielding Graduate University. The program is delivered completely online and thus differs from many of the other programs offered by the university. As a result, a different way to evaluate faculty performance was needed, and the faculty took charge of the process, which resulted in a comprehensive portfolio review.

## MASTER OF ORGANIZATION MANAGEMENT AND DEVELOPMENT (OMD) FACULTY ASSESSMENT AND DEVELOPMENT PROCESS

### Portfolio Process

Each faculty member on continuing appointment will maintain a portfolio concerning his or her work as a faculty member at Fielding Graduate University during at least the previous three years or for as many of the previous quarters of the previous three years as he or she has taught in the OMD curriculum. The Program Director may also require that adjunct and visiting faculty seeking reappointment maintain portfolios. Faculty members will present to the OMD faculty during session for peer learning, collaboration, and feedback once every three years. One faculty member's portfolio will be presented in a collaborative faculty development session at each faculty retreat.

The faculty member's portfolio includes

- A self-evaluation by the faculty member for the past three academic years that the person has taught at Fielding for at least one quarter each year.
- Course evaluations of the faculty member by Fielding Graduate University students of the faculty member.
- Course syllabi and descriptions connected with the faculty member's teaching at Fielding Graduate University.
- Descriptions of the faculty member's participation in university affairs.
- Description of the faculty member's conference presentations, publications, and professional and collaborative development activities.
- Any other material that the faculty member wishes to include.

### Criteria for Evaluation

- *Teaching.* A faculty member should teach well. Evidence of effective teaching will be demonstrated in student program learning assessments, master's projects, and course work. Some but not all indications of such teaching are the development of
  - Scholar-practitioner
  - Critical thinking
  - Stakeholder analysis
  - Practical application
  - Collaboration focus
  - Literature review
  - Dialectical argumentation

    - Comparing and contrasting
    - Synthesis
    - Use of heuristics—sourcing, corroboration, contextualization
- Contributing to the learning environment in programs through designing and executing parts of a curriculum, subject matter expertise, interdisciplinary approaches to material, ability to advise students, facilitation of a stimulating and challenging atmosphere, innovative work in face-to-face sessions, course revisions, and effective sponsorship of individual contracts and internships.
- Fostering students' intellectual and cognitive development.
- Fostering students' communication abilities.
- Displaying intellectual vitality.
- *Meeting commitments.* A faculty member should regularly and cooperatively meet commitments made to students, colleagues, staff, and the college, as judged by peers, students, the deans, and provost. These commitments include, but are not limited to
    - Meeting teaching and session requirements
    - Adhering to course syllabi and curriculum planning obligations
    - Submitting grades for each student at the end of each quarter
- *Planning curriculum.* A faculty member should contribute effectively and cooperatively to curriculum planning as judged by his or her peers, students, the deans, and provost. Curriculum planning can be done in many ways, including
    - Planning academic courses, contributing to program design as well as execution
    - Participating in the development of a coherent and innovative curriculum for certificate programs, session planning, or conference participation
- *Participating in University affairs.* A faculty member may contribute to the university community in such ways as serving on committees and participating in the hiring process, and other ways as reasonably requested and as consistent with effective teaching. The value of

such contributions should be clearly evident in community and financial recognition.

## Professional Development and Collaborative Development

- *Professional development.* A faculty member should continue his or her professional development as evidenced by new learning in Fielding University and, if appropriate, as evidenced in the member's independent work.
- *Collaborative development.* We will use two faculty retreats per year to pursue collaborative faculty development. Collaborative faculty development will include
  - Sharing practices
  - Assessing practices
  - Devising new practices

Our goals are to more effectively support each other through

- Setting up forums of practice
- Making available tools and toolkits
- Sharing practices
- Acknowledging and leveraging faculty expertise
- Developing coaching or training model for the first-term faculty
- Creating new faculty orientation
- Creating an ongoing course in course facilitation
- Conducting faculty sessions that emphasize effective practices
- Making course revisions
- Developing rubrics as jumping-off points for development

## Program Director Responsibilities

- Notify faculty within ninety days that their portfolios are due and write a summary after the completion of the review process.
- Review student evaluations for individual courses taught by the faculty to be used for feedback and development purposes.

- Formally review one course every two years for each faculty member, looking for student learning indicants in the students' papers (critical thinking, scholar or practitioner, stakeholder analysis, student program learning assessment) and collective faculty goal achievement and consistency using the following criteria for patterns of
  - Appropriate responses to students
  - Assigned current-value books (not out of print, too old, too many, too costly, or inaccessible)
  - Value-added participation and appropriate presence
  - Organized or readily understandable syllabi and courses
  - Courses that are group or collaboration focused
  - Discussions facilitated to take students to deeper level
  - Efficient management of courses (such as employing the 80/20 principle)
  - Creation of an adequate context and environment for collaboration

---

# ADDITIONAL RESOURCES

The following resources—including books, websites, and articles—can assist with the assessment function.

## INSTRUCTIONAL DESIGN

Portland State University Instructional Design Handbook.
www.psuonline.pdx.edu/docs/id_handbook.htm#assessment

This site contains many good ideas for transitioning a face-to-face course for online delivery and developing learning objectives, as well as software recommendations for course development, and assessment ideas.

Vidakovic, D., Bevis, J., & Alexander, M. (2004). Bloom's Taxonomy in Developing Assessment Items.
http://mathdl.maa.org/mathDL/4/?pa=content&sa=viewDocument&nodeId=504

This article discusses assessment of math concepts and the development of math courses based on the use of Bloom's Taxonomy.

Michigan Community College Virtual Learning Collaborative.
www.mccvlc.org/~staff/Course-Guidelines-Rubric-v1.2.html#assessment

The Michigan Community College Virtual Learning Collaborative presents guidelines and a rubric for online course development. The rubric contains a scoring guide for course evaluation purposes and a section evaluating online assessments.

## ASSESSMENT DEVELOPMENT

Field-Tested Learning Assessment Guide (FLAG).
www.flaguide.org/

The FLAG offers assessment techniques, including concept mapping, for math, science, engineering, and technology instructors.

University of Maryland University College Assessment Resource Center.
www.umuc.edu/distance/odell/irahe/arc/6too.html

The Assessment Resource Center contains discussion about the assessment process and offers links to several assessment tools, including tools for creation of exams, surveys, and the like.

Cromwell, S. (2006). Assessment Reform: Are We Making Progress?
www.educationworld.com/a_admin/admin/admin059.shtml

This article reviews studies on assessment reform in the K–12 schools. It also contains links to sites that discuss assessment reform and presents alternatives.

University of Wisconsin-Stout Online Assessment Resources.
www.uwstout.edu/soe/profdev/assess.shtml

This site provides links to articles and resources on the development and use of authentic assessments, performance assessments, portfolios, and rubric development.

## AUTHENTIC ASSESSMENT

Authentic Assessment Toolbox.
http://jonathan.mueller.faculty.noctrl.edu/toolbox/index.htm

This site is an online text for the creation and delivery of authentic assessments. In addition, sample rubrics are provided, with guidelines for scoring and grading authentic assessments. Forms of authentic assessment are also presented.

## BLOGS AND WIKIS

The following are some of the numerous sites available in the public domain for the creation of blogs:
www.blogger.com

www.blogspot.com
www.squarespace.com

The following are available for the creation of wikis:
www.wetpaint.com
www.wikiea.com
www.pbwiki.com

## RUBRICS AND RUBRIC DEVELOPMENT

University of Calgary Teaching and Learning Centre.
http://tlc.ucalgary.ca/resources/library/itbl/rubrics-for-student-assignments/rubrics-for-student-assignments.pdf

This site presents material on rubric development along with tips for their use and links to other similar sites.

## PEER REVIEW AND ASSESSMENT

Calibrated Peer Review (CPR).
http://cpr.molsci.ucla.edu/

The homepage of the CPR site states,

> Calibrated Peer Review (CPR)™ is a Web-based program that enables frequent writing assignments even in large classes with limited instructional resources. In fact, CPR can reduce the time an instructor now spends reading and assessing student writing.
>
> CPR offers instructors the choice of creating their own writing assignments or using the rapidly expanding assignment library. Although CPR stems from a science-based model, CPR has the exciting feature that it is discipline independent and level independent.
>
> CPR funding has been generously provided by the National Science Foundation and by the Howard Hughes Medical Institute.

University of Calgary Teaching and Learning Centre.
http://tlc.ucalgary.ca/resources/library/itbl/improving-writing-through-peer-review/improving-writing-through-peer-review

This site reviews the peer review process and provides tips for using peer assessment and links to other like sites.

Gehringer, E. (2000). Strategies and Mechanisms for Electronic Peer Review. North Carolina State University.
http://fie.engrng.pitt.edu/fie2000/papers/1189.pdf

This journal article, published at the October 2000 Frontiers in Education Conference, discusses strategies and mechanisms for electronic peer review. It outlines a peer-grading system for review of student assignments over the World Wide Web called Peer Grader. The system allows authors and reviewers to communicate and authors to update their submissions. This system facilitates collaborative learning and makes it possible to break up a large project into smaller portions. The article summarizes a unique and innovative method of peer review.

The Foundation Coalition.
www.foundationcoalition.org/publications/brochures/2002peer_assessment.pdf

This helpful article provides case examples on the use of peer review, along with grading tips, issues, and concerns, and suggested ways to use peer review.

University of Hawaii at Macronnoa.
http://mwp01.mwp.hawaii.edu/resources/peer_review.htm

This helpful site not only discusses the peer review process but also provides sample feedback forms with suggestions to instructors who want to develop their own.

University of Richmond Writing Center Peer Editing Guide.
http://writing2.richmond.edu/writing/wweb/peeredit.html

The Peer Editing Guide contains specific suggestions for students who are conducting peer reviews on the papers of other students.

## SELF-ASSESSMENT

Student Assessment of Learning Gains.
www.wcer.wisc.edu/salgains/instructor/default.asp

The homepage of the SALG site states,

> This *free* site is designed for instructors of all disciplines who would like feedback from their students about how the course elements are helping their students to learn. It is offered as a service to the

college-level teaching community. Once you've registered, you can do the following both quickly and easily:

- Modify the SALG instrument so that it fits your own course design
- Enable your students to complete this instrument on-line
- Review and download a statistical analysis of the students' responses

## TEST AND QUIZ DEVELOPMENT

Respondus.
www.respondus.com

Respondus is a software application that supports test and quiz development and provides test banks. It can be used with most course management systems. In addition, the company provides Study Mate Author, which allows for the construction of games and other course activities.

Lesson Builder.
www.softchalk.com

Lesson Builder is a content authoring tool that also allows for the creation of tests and quizzes to support the developed content. It can be used with any course management system.

Computer Assessment Centre.
http://caacentre.lboro.ac.uk/resources/web/onlres4.shtml

This site highlights research completed on the use of computer-assisted assessment in universities in Great Britain. Many of the software applications cited are useful in the design and review of assessment activities.

Northern Arizona University Office of Academic Assessment.
www4.nau.edu/assessment/main/research/webtools.htm

This site compiles and presents assessment tools and course evaluation tools, most of which are useable at no charge.

Caveon.
www.caveon.com

Caveon provides web-based security testing services for a fee.

Kryterion.
www.kryteriononline.com

Kryterion provides test development, security, and virtual proctoring services for a fee.

## PORTFOLIO ASSESSMENT

Indiana University – Portfolio Assessment.
www.indiana.edu/~reading/ieo/bibs/portfoli.html

This page contains a bibliography of resources in portfolio assessment.

Alverno College – Diagnostic Digital Portfolio.
http://ddp.alverno.edu/

Alverno College has developed a web-based portfolio tool for the construction and assessment of portfolios. It is available for downloading from the Alverno site.

## COURSE EVALUATION

Rubric for Online Instruction – Chico State University.
www.csuchico.edu/celt/roi/

This site was designed to answer the question, "What does a high-quality online course look like?" It contains a rubric for course evaluation as well as examples of exemplary courses developed using the rubric as a guide.

Checklist for Evaluating Online Courses – Southern Regional Education Board (SREB).
www.sreb.org

This checklist, based on the SREB report on standards for quality online education, is designed to assist schools and colleges in evaluating the quality and effectiveness of their online courses.

## PROGRAM EVALUATION

Quality Matters.
www.qualitymatters.org/

The Quality Matters project is "creating an inter-institutional continuous improvement model for assessing and assuring the quality of online courses." Original project partners include nineteen Maryland Online Community Colleges.

Rubrics and resources have been highlighted by the project planners. Quality Matters offers institutional subscriptions, training, and a range of fee-based services.

EduTools.
www.edutools.info/index.jsp?pj=1

EduTools provides independent reviews, side-by-side comparisons, and consulting services to assist decision making in the e-learning community. Included are categories for course management systems and online course evaluations, as well as other research projects. In the online course evaluation section, users may search by course, subject, grade level, and other categories. This free resource is owned and operated by the Western Cooperative for Educational Telecommunications (WCET).

## GENERAL ASSESSMENT RESOURCES

North Carolina State University – Online Assessment Resources.
www2.acs.ncsu.edu/UPA/assmt/resources.htm

This site contains links to numerous sites, articles, and resources related to assessment in both face-to-face and online environments.

# REFERENCES


Achtemeier, S., Morris, L., & Finnegan, C. (2003, February). Considerations for Developing Evaluations of Online Courses. *JALN,* 7(1), 1–13. Retrieved from [http://www.aln.org/publications/jaln/v7n1/pdf/v7n1_achtemeier.pdf].

American Psychological Association. (2007). Understanding Assessment. Retrieved from Assessment CyberGuide [http://www.apa.org/ed/guidehomepage.html].

Angelo, T., & Cross, K. P. (1993). *Classroom Assessment Techniques.* San Francisco: Jossey-Bass.

Arbaugh, J. B. (2000). How Classroom Environment and Student Engagement Affect Learning in Internet-Based MBA Courses. *Business Communication Quarterly, 63*(4), 9–26.

Bachman, L. (2000). Foreword to G. Ekbatani and H. DeLeon Pierson, *Learner-Directed Assessment in ESL.* Hillsdale, NJ: Erlbaum.

Banta, T. (2003). Introduction: Why Portfolios? In T. Banta (Ed.), *Portfolio Assessment: Uses, Cases, Scoring, and Impact.* Assessment Update Collections. San Francisco: Jossey-Bass.

Barnett, R. (1990). *The Idea of Higher Education.* Milton Keynes, UK: SRHE and Open University Press.

Bloom, B. S., & Krathwohl, D. R. (1956). Taxonomy of Educational Objectives: The Classification of Educational Goals, by a Committee of College and University Examiners. *Handbook 1: Cognitive Domain.* New York: Longmans.

Brookfield, S. D. (1995). *Becoming a Critically Reflective Teacher.* San Francisco: Jossey-Bass.

Brooks, J., & Brooks, M. (1993). *In Search of Understanding: The Case for Constructivist Classrooms.* Alexandria, VA: Association for Supervision and Curriculum Development.

Buzzetto-More, N., & Alade, A. (2006). Best Practices in E-Assessment. *Journal of Information Technology Education, 5.* Retrieved from [http://jite.org/documents/Vol5/v5p251–269Buzzetto152.pdf].

Byers, C. (2002, May/June). Interactive Assessment and Course Transformation Using Web-Based Tools. Retrieved from *The Technology Source* [http://ts.mivu.org/default.asp?show=article&id=928].

Case, R. (2008, January-February). Independent Learning and Test Question Development: The Intersection of Student and Content. *Assessment Update, 20*(1), 5–7.

Chickering, A. W., & Gamson, Z. F. (1987). Seven Principles for Good Practice in Undergraduate Education. *AAHE Bulletin, 39*(7), 3–6.

Conrad, R. M., & Donaldson, A. (2004). *Engaging the Online Learner: Activities and Resources for Creative Instruction.* San Francisco: Jossey-Bass.

Cranton, P. (1994). *Understanding and Promoting Transformative Learning: A Guide for Educators of Adults.* San Francisco: Jossey-Bass.

DePaul University. (2007). Faculty Peer Evaluation of Online Teaching. Retrieved from [http://www.snl.depaul.edu/contents/current/forms/faculty_peer_evaluation_of_online_teaching.doc].

Dunn, L., Parry, S., & Morgan, C. (2002). Seeking Quality in Criterion Referenced Assessment, *Education Line.* Retrieved from ProQuest Education Database.

Dunn, L., Morgan, C., O'Reilly, M., & Parry, S. (2004). *The Student Assessment Handbook: New Directions in Traditional & Online Assessment.* London: RoutledgeFarmer.

Fink, L. D. (n.d.). Significant Learning: A Taxonomy for Identifying Important Kinds of Learning. Retrieved from Northcentral University Faculty Resources.

Gaytan, J. (2005, Spring). Effective Assessment Techniques for Online Instruction. *Information Technology, Learning, and Performance Journal, 23*(1), 25–33.

Gaytan, J., & McEwan, B. C. (2007). Effective Online Instructional and Assessment Strategies. *The American Journal of Distance Education, 21*(3), 117–132.

Graham, C., Cagiltay, K, Lim, B., Craner, J., & Duffy, T. (2001, March/April). Seven Principles of Effective Teaching: A Practical Lens for Evaluating Online Courses. *The Technology Source Archives at the University of North Carolina,* March/April 2001. Retrieved from [http://technologysource.org/article/seven_principles_of_effective_teaching/].

Hase, S., & Kenyon, C. (2000, December). From Andragogy to Heutagogy. *UltiBASE Articles.* Retrieved from [http://ultibase.rmit.edu.au/Articles/dec00/hase2.htm].

Huba, M. E., & Freed, J. (2000). *Learner-Centered Assessment on College Campuses: Shifting the Focus from Teaching to Learning.* Needham Heights, MA: Allyn & Bacon.

Illinois Online Network. (n.d.). Strategies to Minimize Cheating Online. *Online Education Resources.* Retrieved from [http://www.ion.uillinois.edu/resources/tutorials/assessment/cheating.asp].

Johnson, D., Wilkes, F., Ormond, P., & Figueroa, R. (2002). Adding Value to the IS'97 . . . Curriculum Models: An Interactive Visualization and Analysis Prototype. *Journal of*

*Information Systems Education, 13*(2), 135–142. Retrieved from [http://www.zeang.com/robertfig/JSIE-IS971.pdf].

Jonassen, D., Davidson, M., Collins, M., Campbell, J., & Haag, B. (1995). Constructivism and Computer-Mediated Communication in Distance Education, *The American Journal of Distance Education, 9*(2), 7–26.

Jones, E. A., Voorhees, R. A., & Paulson, K. (2002). *Defining and Assessing Learning: Exploring Competency-Based Initiatives.* Washington, DC: National Center for Education Statistics.

Knowles, M. S. (1973; 1990). *The Adult Learner: A Neglected Species* (4th ed.). Houston: Gulf Publishing.

Kolitch, E., & Dean, A. V. (1999). Student Ratings of Instruction in the USA: Hidden Assumptions and Missing Conceptions about "Good" Teaching. *Studies in Higher Education, 24*(1), 27–43.

Lynch, K., Goold, A., & Blain, J. (2004). Students' Pedagogical Preferences in the Delivery of IT Capstone Courses. *Issues in Informing Science and Information Technology.* Retrieved from [http://proceedings.informingscience.org/InSITE2004/067lynch.pdf].

Magennis, S., & Farrell, A. (2005). Teaching and Learning Activities: Expanding the Repertoire to Support Student Learning. In G. O'Neill, S. Moore, & B. McMullin (Eds.), *Emerging Issues in the Practice of University Learning and Teaching.* Dublin: AISHE.

Major, H., & Taylor, D. (2003). Teaching for Learning: Design and Delivery of Community College Courses. *The Community College Enterprise, 9*(2), 85.

Mandernach, B. J., Donnelli, E., Dailey, A., & Schulte, M. (2005). A Faculty Evaluation Model for Online Instructors: Mentoring and Evaluation in the Online Classroom. *Online Journal of Distance Education Administration, VIII*(III), State University of West Georgia Distance Education Center. Retrieved on January 1, 2008, from [http://www.westga.edu/~distance/ojdla/fall83/mandernach83.html].

McNett, M. (2002, May/June). Curbing Academic Dishonesty in Online Courses. *Pointers and Clickers.* Illinois Online Network. Retrieved from [http://www.ion.uillinois.edu/resources/pointersclickers/2002_05/index.asp].

McVay Lynch, M. (2002). *The Online Educator: A Guide to Creating the Virtual Classroom.* London: RoutledgeFalmer.

Mehrotra, D. (n.d.). Applying Total Quality Management in Academics. Retrieved from [http://www.isixsigma.com/library/content/c020626a.asp].

Michigan State University. (2005). Pedagogy and Techniques. Retrieved on December 23, 2007, from [http://teachvu.vu.msu.edu/public/pedagogy/assessment/index.php?].

Milam, J., Voorhees, R., & Bedard-Voorhees, A. (2004, Summer). Assessment of Online Education: Policies, Practices, and Recommendations. In A. M. Serban & J. Friedlander (Eds.), *Developing and Implementing Assessment of Student Learning Outcomes.* New Directions for Community Colleges, No. 126. San Francisco: Jossey-Bass.

Morgan, C., & O'Reilly, M. (1999). *Assessing Open and Distance Learners.* London: Kogan Page.

Myers, C., & Jones, T. (1993). *Promoting Active Learning: Strategies for the College Classroom.* San Francisco: Jossey-Bass.

Palloff, R. M., & Pratt, K. (2003). *The Virtual Student: A Profile and Guide.* San Francisco: Jossey-Bass.

Palloff, R. M., & Pratt, K. (2005). *Collaborating Online: Learning Together in Community.* San Francisco: Jossey-Bass.

Palloff, R. M., & Pratt, K. (2007). *Building Online Learning Communities: Effective Strategies for the Virtual Classroom.* San Francisco: Jossey-Bass.

Rasmussen, K. L., & Northrup, P. T. (1999). Interactivity: Strategies that Facilitate Instructor-Student Communication. *World Conference on Educational Multimedia, Hypermedia and Telecommunications, 1999*(1), 1243–1244.

Roberts, T. G., Irani, T. A., Telg, R. W., & Lundy, L. K. (2005). The Development of an Instrument to Evaluate Distance Education Courses Using Student Attitudes. *The American Journal of Distance Education, 19*(1), 55–64.

Roblyer, M. D., & Wiencke, W. R. (2003). Design and Use of a Rubric to Assess and Encourage Interactive Qualities in Distance Courses. *The American Journal of Distance Education, 17*(2), 77–98.

Rowe, N. C. (2004). Cheating in Online Student Assessment: Beyond Plagiarism. *Online Journal of Distance Learning Administration, VII*(II). State University of West Georgia Distance Education Center. Retrieved from [http://www.westga.edu/%7Edistance/ojdla/summer72/rowe72.html].

Sewell, M., Marczac, M., & Horn, M. (n.d.). *The Use of Portfolio Assessment in Evaluation.* University of Arizona CYFERNet. Retrieved from [http://ag.arizona.edu/fcs/cyfernet/cyfar/Portfo%7E3.htm].

Speck, B. W. (2002). Learning-Teaching Assessment Paradigms and the On-Line Classroom. In R. S. Anderson, J. Bauer, & B. W. Speck (Eds.), *Assessment Strategies for the On-line Class: From Theory to Practice.* San Francisco: Jossey-Bass.

Stein, D., & Wanstreet, C. E. (2003). Role of Social Presence, Choice of Online or Face-to-Face Group Format, and Satisfaction with Perceived Knowledge Gained in a Distance Learning Environment. *2003 Midwest Research to Practice Conference in Adult, Continuing, and Community Education.* Retrieved from [http://www.alumni-osu.org/midwest/midwest%20papers/Stein%20&%20Wanstreet—Done.pdf].

Stevens, D. D., & Levi, A. J. (2004). *Introduction to Rubrics: An Assessment Tool to Save Grading Time, Convey Effective Feedback, and Promote Student Learning.* Sterling, VA: Stylus.

Sunal, D. W., Sunal, C. S., Odell, M. R., & Sundberg, C. A. (2003, Summer). Research Supported Best Practices for Developing Online Learning. *The Journal of Interactive Online Learning, 2*(1). Retrieved from [http://www.ncolr.org/].

Tobin, T. (2004). Best Practices for Administrative Evaluation of Online Faculty. *Online Journal of Distance Learning Administration, VII*(II), State University of West Georgia Distance Education Center. Retrieved from [http://www.westga.edu/~distance/ojdla/summer72/tobin72.html].

Varvel, V. (2005). Honesty in Online Education. *Pointers and Clickers, 6*(1). Illinois Online Network. Retrieved from [http://www.ion.uillinois.edu/resources/pointersclickers/2005_01/index.asp].

Walvoord, B. E. (2004). *Assessment Clear and Simple.* San Francisco: Jossey-Bass.

Walvoord, B. E., & Anderson, V. J. (1998). *Effective Grading: A Tool for Learning and Assessment.* San Francisco: Jossey-Bass.

Weimer, M. (2002). *Learner-Centered Teaching: Five Key Changes to Practice.* San Francisco: Jossey-Bass.

Williams, P. E. (2003). Roles and Competencies for Distance Education Programs in Higher Education Institutions. *The American Journal of Distance Education, 17*(1), 45–57.

# INDEX

## D



## E



## F



## G



## H



## I



## J

## Q



## R



## S



## T



## U

## JOSSEY-BASS GUIDES TO ONLINE TEACHING AND LEARNING

***Other books in the best-selling series...***

* **ENGAGING THE ONLINE LEARNER**
**Activities and Resources for Creative Instruction**
By: Rita-Marie Conrad, J. Ana Donaldson
ISBN: 978-0-7879-6667-6 (Paper) • 144 pp. • $27.00

* **EXPLORING THE DIGITAL LIBRARY**
**A Guide for Online Teaching and Learning**
By: Kay Johnson, Elaine Magusin
ISBN: 978-0-7879-7627-9 (Paper) • 176 pp. • $27.00

* **COLLABORATING ONLINE**
**Learning Together in Community**
By: Rena M. Palloff, Keith Pratt
ISBN: 978-0-7879-7614-9 (Paper) • 128 pp. • $27.00

* **LEARNING IN REAL TIME**
**Synchronous Teaching and Learning Online**
By: Jonathan E. Finkelstein
ISBN: 978-0-7879-7921-8 (Paper) • 176 pp. • $27.00

* **CONQUERING THE CONTENT**
**A Step-by-Step Guide to Online Course Design**
By: Robin M. Smith
ISBN: 978-0-7879-9442-6 (Paper) • 176 pp. • $27.00

***AVAILABLE December 2008***

**USING WIKIS FOR ONLINE COLLABORATION**
**The Power of the Read-Write Web**
By: James A. West, Margaret L. West
ISBN: 978-0-470-34333-3 (Paper) • 120 pp. • $27.00

* indicates titles also offered at a <u>*20% discount*</u> ($108.00) bundled together in **The Online Teaching and Learning Tool Kit**, ISBN: 978-0-470-38053-6